BECOME A LIFE
BALANCE MASTER

BECOME A LIFE
BALANCE MASTER

RIC GIARDINA

BEYOND
WORDS
Publishing
I   N   C

Beyond Words Publishing, Inc.
20827 N.W. Cornell Road, Suite 500
Hillsboro, Oregon 97124-9808
503-531-8700

The definitions used as epigraphs for chapters 8 through 15 are from
Webster's Third New International Dictionary, Unabridged, copyright
© 1993 by Merriam-Webster, Inc.

Editor: Julie Steigerwaldt
Proofreader: Marvin Moore
Design: Michelle Farinella
Composition: William H. Brunson Typography Services

Printed in the United States of America
Distributed to the book trade by Publishers Group West

Library of Congress Cataloging-in-Publication Data
Giardina, Ric.
    Become a life balance master / Ric Giardina.
        p.   cm.
    Includes bibliographical references.
    ISBN 1-58270-098-2
    1. Self-actualization (Psychology).   2. Quality of life.   I. Title.
BF637.S4G486   2003
158—dc21

                                                  2003000978

The corporate mission of Beyond Words Publishing, Inc.:
    Inspire to Integrity

For Aunt Vi,
who loved us and laughed with us to the very last.
You will be in our hearts forever.

Life is a process of becoming,
a combination of states we have to go
through. Where people fail is that
they wish to elect a state and remain
in it. This is a kind of death.

◆ ANAÏS NIN
WINTER OF ARTIFICE

CONTENTS

ACKNOWLEDGMENTS   xi
INTRODUCTION   xiii

PART I: YOUR LIFE BALANCE EQUATION

1   WHY BOTHER WITH BALANCE?   3
2   THE FOUR MYTHS OF LIFE BALANCE   13
3   A FEW FUNDAMENTALS   25
4   THE IMPORTANCE OF SUPPORT   45
5   THE HABIT CYCLES   53
6   YOUR LIFE BALANCE CATEGORIES   71
7   THE LIFE BALANCE EQUATION PROCESS   83

PART II: MASTERING LIFE BALANCE

8   THE BALANCE MASTER'S FACTORIAL SYSTEM   107
9   MEDITATE × 7   121
10   ACT × 6   129
11   SOCIALIZE × 5   137
12   TRAIN × 4   145
13   ETHOS × 3   153
14   REFLECT × 2   159
15   SABBATH × 1   169
EPILOGUE   177
NOTES   181

ACKNOWLEDGMENTS

A BOOK LIKE THIS must begin with a statement of gratitude. To that end, I wish to identify those people who have contributed in whatever way to the process that has resulted in this volume being in your hands.

First and foremost I want to acknowledge you, the reader, for reaching the point along your path where you are able to see that your life can be more of what you want than it is now and for recognizing that you have the power to change it. This is the stuff of miracles, and you possess it. (If someone bought this book for you as a gift, thank him or her, but be sure also to acknowledge yourself for bringing into your life someone who cares a great deal about you.)

It is impossible to list all the names of the hundreds of people who have attended my corporate-sponsored and personal workshops on Life Balance throughout the years. Those people have tested this system and have proven to themselves and to me that it works.

This book would still be just a good idea if it weren't for the personal encouragement and support of my friends at Beyond Words. Time and time again they assisted me in getting over the hard spots—both in the writing process and in working the writing into my already overly full life. My sincerest thanks go to Cynthia Black, Richard Cohn, Sylvia Hayse, Beth Hoyt, and most especially to my editor, Julie Steigerwaldt, who has yet again provided a gentle and guiding hand. I recently shocked an author friend of mine by casually mentioning that "I love my publisher!" I wasn't exaggerating—I do!

Marvin Moore did a spectacular job of proofing the manuscript and making suggestions that were both accurate and welcome. As usual, he went beyond our expectations of what proofreaders are supposed to do. Bill Brunson's layout has added a dimension to the finished volume that reflects and reinforces its timeless message.

Quite simply, I would be lost without the unconditional love and support of my wife, best friend, life partner, and certain beyond-this-world soul mate, Betsy. Everyone who meets her makes a point of telling me that she is my best asset—bar none. I might be offended if I didn't know myself that no truer words were ever spoken.

As the final notation, it seems appropriate somehow to mention our daughter, Annalisa, who, even at fifteen years of age, has developed a remarkable sense of Life Balance. Most importantly, she has already acquired the ability to recognize when her life is off-kilter and the talent to take steps to get it back on track. That represents hope to all of us.

INTRODUCTION

> *Living is a thing you do now or never—*
> *which do you?*
> ◆ *PIET HEIN*

ALL MY LIFE I've been something of an overachiever in the sense that there have always been many things in which I've had a great deal of interest. I've also chosen to participate in most of them. That much was apparent when I was just a toddler, and it's formally documented as early as high school: at the back of our yearbook there is a listing of the activities each of the senior-class members participated in during their high school careers. My listing shows eighteen different activities—the most of anyone, and several of those represent two or even three years of participation. As I said, I've always been a very busy guy with immense interest in lots of things.

That didn't change in college, in graduate school, during my first jobs, or any time since either. I'm still engaged in a myriad of activities, many of which require a significant amount of time, discipline, newly learned skills, and dedication. One of my friends introduces me as someone who is not merely multi-dimensional but *over*-dimensional!

It would be too easy to assume that the "jack of all trades, master of none" moniker could be applied to me, but my experiences and successes indicate that this would be inaccurate. Looking back, I think I have done well in so many different disciplines because I somehow inherently developed a way of focusing on one or two areas until there was some appropriate place to shift my attention or until circumstances forced me to break my concentration and move from one thing to another. In short, I have a natural inclination that leans me *toward* balance in my life rather than away from it. I can, as it were, easily juggle many things at one time without having the juggling itself wear on me. It has only been in the last few decades that I have recognized this for the incredible gift that it is.

Indeed, it was only after I began managing other people about midway through my career in corporate America that I began to notice that others—particularly those I supervised, since my managerial style was to get close to them and the totality of their lives—were having trouble keeping their lives in balance.

At first, I simply could not understand this. Most of these people seemed to have far fewer things to do than I did and yet they also appeared to be having a much more difficult time than I was dealing with the demands being made on them. Many couldn't cope at all, and I watched as their families and relationships or their health or their work productivity or any combination of things fell apart around them.

My friends, associates, co-workers, and employees seemed to be victimized by all the things in their lives that were frequently and insistently calling for their attention. In talking with them—actually, more often listening to them vent while they were in the middle of some stressful episode—I was left with the feeling that they had no control over what they did with their time and attention. The people, activities, and even the possessions they'd collected made demands on them, and they were powerless to do anything but react. Life for them became one reaction after another.

They seemed to have no sense of what their lives actually looked like; they could not get out of the details of the trees to see the totality of the forest. More importantly, they seemed to have no plan to move their lives to something that might be better for them and for those in their immediate circles—families, friends, and co-workers.

It occurred to me that I had access to a mind-set and some skills that could be useful to these people. Being involved in many things has required me to develop a disciplined methodology and a construct to hold all the various elements of my life.

I also realized that because I had so many activities in my life in which I had keen and genuine interest, it became nearly impossible for any one of them to push me out of balance. Oh, I might have felt overwhelmed by all there was to do at any given time, but even those occasional periods of overwhelm were somehow themselves balanced. It was never just one thing toward which my life was slipping like some unstoppable avalanche.

The need to keep track of and ensure that I completed each of the tasks for all of the aspects of my life activities ultimately developed into a discipline of sorts, and that discipline required me to make conscious and sometimes difficult choices. No matter how complicated the requirements or the mix became, I seemed able to handle it and rarely felt out of control.

And that's what I brought to many of those conversations with others caught in the throes of imbalance—hope that things could get better for them coupled with specific tools and things to do that would actually effect the changes they could now allow themselves to envision.

What you have here in this book is a remarkable opportunity—perhaps even a "once in a lifetime" opportunity—to take control of your life and to balance it based on a vision that you believe will work for you. It is an opportunity for you to move yourself forward to a Life Balance equation that may be better for you and for everyone around you rather than simply continuing to make the best of what has been dealt to you. Most people don't even know that this is an option. When you've completed this book, you will not only know that it is an option, but you will know exactly how to do it.

SOME THINGS TO CONSIDER

It is probable that this book actually is the set of directions you have been looking for that will allow you to design the life you want to live; indeed, it is intended to be that. It is also possible that this program may not be ideal for you, although I am a firm believer in *kismet*—if you have this book in your hands, it's there for a reason.

But be forewarned: If you intend to get any value from this book, it is not to be taken lightly—nor is it for the fainthearted. What you do with this book and, hence, whether it helps you to change your life for the better or whether it does nothing at all is entirely up to you.

In any event, before you start on this journey, you need to know the following: To get any benefit from this book will require you to embrace and to commit and continuously *recommit* to exhibiting a combination of certain personal characteristics. These characteristics include attention, intention, intuition, creativity, articulation, action, discipline, integrity, and patience.

Attention, because if you have any hope of making changes to the way you are living your life—some people like to say "doing life"— then you will have to start taking a close look at what you are actually doing at the present time. This will require a new level of mindfulness about your thought processes, your choices and decisions, and your actions and activities. Frankly, maintaining that level of awareness can seem forced in the best of circumstances and is likely to make you uncomfortable at times.

Intention, because at every stage of this journey it will be necessary for you to be clear about the direction into which you want to move next. If you don't know where you are going, how will you know when or if you have gotten there? Intention is like keeping your eye on the ball. It is also like a welcome fire in your soul that you can stoke from time to time to get you over the rough spots.

Intuition, because there will be times when things will *look* like they are moving in the right direction, but something inside you may be trying to tell you that something is off. You will need to learn to listen to those little messages—those suggestions, inklings, pictures, and nudges from your subconscious. Frequently, your subconscious mind knows more about what is going on in your "real" world than your conscious mind does. If you fail to heed your intuition, you will end up traveling down too many dark alleys and dead ends in your quest to make your life one of balance.

Creativity, because this journey will require you to look at your life in different ways and to come up with alternative solutions to the issues and problems you have been attempting to solve by making the same choices over and over and expecting different results. Those choices haven't worked to give you what you truly want in the past, and they will not work to provide you with your heart's desire for the future. The path to your balanced future begins with you reaching deep into your creative self for new approaches and ways of being that will surprise you in terms of their depth, their appropriateness, and the results that they bring.

Articulation, because as you begin to change the world around you beginning with your views of your self, your life activities, and your responsibilities, it will become necessary for you to explain to those who are in your circle of family, friends, and business associates—and most of all those who rely on you—that you are undertaking to change the way you are living your life. You need to do this for two reasons: First, because it is unfair to surprise people with unexpected behaviors. If you have been living life a particular way and then suddenly change your behavior without giving notice of your intentions to the people in your life, they may respond badly. Second, because you will want to garner support for your new way of living, and you can only get that by explaining what you are doing and why.

Action, because planning to do something is not the same thing as doing it. Our dreams become realities only to the extent that we actually start doing something about making them happen. For you to succeed on this journey, you will need to be action-oriented in a very deliberate and mindful way.

Discipline, because taking mindful action one or two times is not enough any more than running a mile or two would prepare you for a marathon. To change what you are doing *consistently* for the long haul, the new actions that you do only deliberately and mindfully at first will need to become your unconscious default actions—your new habits. To accomplish this, it will be necessary for you to be disciplined in both constancy and repetition.

Integrity, because you will undermine your entire program if you fudge your self-assessment and your progress and if you are anything other than ruthlessly honest with yourself. For many people, this is the hardest characteristic to embrace. After all, most people get off balance because they either haven't been paying attention to the consequences of their behaviors, choices, and actions or because, even if they do begin to recognize subliminal stirrings that things aren't right, they fool themselves into thinking that everything will work itself out without the need to make any changes. This is yet one more example of our human tendency to do the same thing over and over with the ridiculous expectation that at some point we will get a different result.

Patience, finally, because whatever the state of your life and your Life Balance equation at this point, you have arrived here through the making of choices and the taking of actions over a lengthy period of time—perhaps your entire life. You will not be able to suddenly shift direction in the blink of an eye and start down a direct course to your heart's desire. As noted above, it will take disciplined repetition of mindful choices as well as actions taken in full awareness of their consequences over a period of time to change what have effectively become your habits. There will be times that you succeed and times that you do not. You will need to practice patience in good measure—with the process, with other people in your life, and most importantly, with yourself—as day by day you make different choices, try alternative approaches, monitor your progress, and then reclaim your chosen path when you have discovered you have somehow strayed from it.

If you believe you meet the requirements above, if you are sure that this book is a good one for you to use at this point in your life, and if you are ready, we can proceed.

WHAT THIS BOOK CAN DO FOR YOU

This book is written in two parts that are related but at the same time independent of each other. It is possible that you could spend quite some time—a year or more!—learning the elements of the first part of this book and applying the tenets to creating and then maintaining a level of Life Balance which represents what you want in life. At some point, as a balanced life becomes your standard stock in trade—your default way of living—you may discover that it is time for you to move on to the second part, which explains how to develop mastery over Life Balance. It is also possible that you will move quickly through the first part—either because your life is already significantly in balance or because you are able to successfully put these concepts to work—and that you will want to move into mastery of Life Balance immediately. This book will accommodate any pace with which you are comfortable. Here is an overview of the two parts.

The first part, "Your Life Balance Equation," covers the essentials of Life Balance, including why Life Balance is important, some commonly held misconceptions about Life Balance and about how to achieve it, and a few fundamental concepts that will be used throughout the rest of this book. You will understand how the Existing Habit

Cycle dictates how you live your life day to day and influences the choices you make and the results you achieve. More than just learning how to overcome the possible negative effects of the Existing Habit Cycle, you will learn how to use the Habit Creation Cycle to turn your penchant for creating habits to your advantage and reap the benefits of harnessing their power—power that, up until now, has likely been locking you in place and preventing you from reaching your full potential. You will learn a very simple but remarkably effective process for determining where you are in your path toward greater Life Balance as well as a fail-safe course-correction mechanism that will keep you moving ever closer to your goal. We will also discuss the need for ongoing personal support in this effort and how best to get it.

The second part of this book, "Mastering Life Balance," is for those who feel that they have achieved a significant level of success using the more general process of creating and maintaining a suitable Life Balance equation from the first part of the book and who are interested in developing a level of mastery.

Although it requires a great deal of work in terms of intention and attention, the results of Life Balance Mastery can be spectacular. Those who practice Life Balance at the level of Mastery reach unparalleled levels of achievement in their lives in many aspects, including spiritual development, relationships, careers, finances, health and fitness, connection to their communities, and an overall sense of well-being.

Part II also discusses the Balance Master's Factorial System, which is a methodology and template I have developed over the last decade that allows you to monitor your progress on a daily, weekly, monthly, and yearly basis in several key areas. This model allows you maximum flexibility and is personally adjustable to the particular circumstances of your life. It is a visual and a visceral system in that it relies heavily on a graphic representation of your progress and engages your intuition about what you are doing on a daily basis and why.

Part II contains a chapter on each element of the Balance Master's Factorial System. This model works and can produce remarkable results in your life if you are disciplined in using it. Like all things in life, your results will be directly proportional to your levels of commitment and mindful activity.

There is plenty of time, however, before you decide whether you want to make an effort to move into Mastery of Life Balance—and much to do between now and then. It's important to recognize that significant changes can be made in your life and in your relationships by applying even a few of the principles and techniques available to you in this book. You can always come back again later with the intention of moving yourself to your next level.

Let's get started.

PART I

YOUR LIFE BALANCE EQUATION

1

Why Bother with Balance?

SOMETHING AT OUR MOST INNER CORE tells us that balance in life is important. Indeed, we may notice this only when we are *off* balance and begin reaping the results of having been off balance for some lengthy period of time, at which point it is often too late. Nevertheless, on some nonphysical plane we seem to have a mechanism similar to the physical mechanism in the inner ear that tells us when we are off balance with the physical world and that gives us the opportunity to correct our position gravitationally before we stumble or fall.

Too frequently, however, we fail to heed the warnings of this Life Balance monitoring mechanism, and the results are loss of health, loss of relationships, loss of productivity, loss of aliveness and authenticity, and, most ironically, frequently the loss of the very things—job, family, friends—for which we might believe we allowed ourselves to go out of balance in the first place.

Balance is, after all, the natural state of the universe. Even water seeks its own level. There have been hundreds of studies of ecological balance around the globe and of the local disasters that occur when that balance is disrupted by the introduction of some new species foreign to the locality. Examples of this phenomenon include zebra mussels, gypsy moths, mute swans, nutria, the water chestnut, purple loosestrife, and the kudzu vine. Each of these animal and plant species had an appropriate niche in its own ecological system, but their introductions into foreign ecologies have been nothing short of catastrophic: Non-native species spread rapidly because the predatory checks and balances of their native ecologies are missing, and they then displace native plants and animals further up the food chain—including endangered species.

Indeed, you may remember the balance upset recently caused by the northern snakehead (*Channa argus*), a top-level predator fish native to China that was found in a small pond in Crofton, Maryland. It was dubbed the "Frankenfish" by the press because of its uncanny ability to breathe air and travel short distances over dry land. When an unwitting local resident released into a pond two specimens that had grown too large for his aquarium, the pond's ecological balance was upset. Northern snakeheads are large predators that can affect the populations of other fish, amphibians, and invertebrates. The nearby Little Patuxent River hosts endangered fish species and recovering populations of anadromous fish (e.g., shad) that could be threatened by the establishment of populations of snakeheads if the pond spilled over into the river during heavy rain. In the end, authorities decided to kill all the vegetation in the pond by the application of herbicides, thus starving the animal life of oxygen, and then to complete the elimination of the snakehead—and all the other native species of animals and plants—by releasing poison into the pond. They plan to restock the pond when it is certain that no snakeheads are remaining.[1] In some situations, balance is everything.

Consider that even the stars and planets operate in balance. Look at the way our own planet travels through space. As the earth makes its way around the sun, there are four milestones we recognize as special events, and that recognition itself is based on the balanced relationship these events have with each other. Two of these are in complete balance because they are equivalent although opposites—the vernal equinox and the autumnal equinox. The vernal equinox (approximately March 21) occurs when the sun crosses the equator from south to north; the autumnal equinox (approximately September 23) occurs when the sun crosses the equator from north to south. From a balance perspective, what makes these two events interesting is that when each one occurs, the length of the light of day and the dark of night are *exactly* the same on both days even though the events occur opposite each other on the celestial calendar and in space.

The other two events—the summer and winter solstices—are in balance as well. During the summer solstice, the sun reaches its greatest declination at exactly $23\frac{1}{2}$ degrees north of the equator, and during the winter solstice, the sun reaches its greatest declination south of the equator also at exactly $23\frac{1}{2}$ degrees.

We see similar examples of balance at the atomic and molecular levels. Every stable atom and every molecule is in balance with the total number of negatively charged electrons equaling the total number of positively charged protons. In those cases in which a particular element or molecule is not in such balance, there is instability, and the atom or molecule begins spewing electrons or other subatomic particles in an effort to achieve balance. Alternatively, the unstable atom or molecule combines with some other out-of-balance atom or molecule to achieve balance through ionic or covalent bonding.

Despite what we may think or like to think about our role in nature, we humans are part of a balanced universe, and it is natural for us to be in balance and, conversely, unnatural for us to be out of balance in our lives.

This, of course, raises the question as to why it is that we don't live our lives in a state of balance like the universe around us. The quick answer is that we have attempted to remove ourselves from the natural order of things. Why has this happened to us? Again, the quick answer is that our approach to living has traditionally been a left-brain, cognitive, logical one. Relying so heavily on the left brain in our history of evolution has given us the *appearance* of having successfully removed ourselves from the natural order of things. The truth, however, is that we have lost our way. What, if anything, can be done about it?

The only solution is an active one that incorporates all of the elements—physical, mental, emotional, and spiritual—that identify us as human beings. Each of us must take stock of what we are actually doing with our time, examine that information to determine how it fits with how we want to spend our lifetimes, apply a significant amount of right-brain thinking (read: "feeling") and intuitive process to what we find, and then make adjustments to bring our realities more in line with our heartfelt desires and expectations.

At this point you may be thinking, "All very interesting, but why is this concept of balance so important?" The answer to that question in one word is *stress*!

Some twenty years ago, the cover story for *Time* magazine's June 6, 1983, issue called stress "The Epidemic of the Eighties" and referred to it as our leading health problem. And the situation has most certainly gotten worse since then.

Everywhere evidence is building that stress is on the increase. Numerous surveys indicate that adult Americans perceive that they are under significantly more stress than a decade or two ago. In 1996, *Prevention* magazine reported the results of a survey which found that almost 75 percent of respondents felt that they experience "great stress" one day a week, while one out of three stated that they feel this way more than twice each week. When that same survey was done in 1983, only 55 percent of the respondents reported feeling under great stress on a weekly basis. While job stress is certainly the leading cause of stress for adults, stress levels have also escalated in children, teenagers, college students, and the elderly.[2]

For thousands of years people believed that stress would make people sick. Up until the nineteenth century, the belief that one's passions and emotions were intimately linked to disease or wellness was fairly well established. Doctors frequently sent ill patients to mountain spas and seaside resorts to recover from illness, the theory being that a change in location and climate would reduce a patient's stress levels and, therefore, cure his ills.

As medical science progressed and tangible causes were discovered for one illness after another, the theory of stress causing disease gradually lost favor and was soon nearly forgotten. It seems we have come full circle with respect to the negative impact of stress on the human body. In the last few decades, the connection between stress and the human immune system has been the subject of much research at the National Institute of Mental Health (NIMH) and at other major medical research facilities.

So, why exactly is stress bad for the body? Think of it this way. The human body's response to stress is not unlike a jet airplane readying for a takeoff. Every engine, monitoring, and control system is revved to the maximum in preparation for the takeoff. During times of stress, virtually every system in the body—the heart and blood vessels, the immune system, the lungs, the digestive system, all the sensory organs, and the brain and nervous system—is modified by the release of hormones and other secretions to meet the perceived danger.

Danger? What danger? you might ask.

It is important to understand that the human response to stress is preprogrammed biologically and was undoubtedly designed and refined to deal with our most important stressors as hunters and gatherers: the occasional confrontation with a saber-toothed tiger, a member of a hostile tribe, or some other threat to life and limb.

The nature of this reaction is that stress sets off an alarm in the brain, which then responds by preparing the body for defensive action of one type or another. This is commonly known as the "fight or flight" response. The nervous system is aroused and hormones are released into the bloodstream. The effect of these hormones on the body is significant. The heart rate and blood pressure increase dramatically to enhance the flow of blood to the brain to improve decision-making ability. Blood-sugar levels are raised as the body immediately begins breaking down stored glycogen, fat, and protein to ensure there is sufficient fuel for the fight or the flight. The lungs begin to breathe in air more deeply to make certain there is an ample supply of oxygen. Blood is shunted away from the digestive tract, where digestion is no longer a primary concern, to the large muscles of the legs and arms to provide both strength in the case of combat or speed in the case of flight. The body even anticipates injury and prepares to contain damage by adjusting the blood chemistry so as to provide for quicker clotting to prevent excessive blood loss in the case of lacerations or internal hemorrhaging.[3]

The good news is that we no longer have to deal with saber-toothed tigers. The bad news is that our bodies are still reacting to stress *of any type* as though we were, in fact, facing that proverbial tiger! Even when the stress results from something relatively benign such as getting stuck in traffic, having a few "words" with someone at the office, time crunches, running late, or any of a host of other psychological threats that plague modern humans in our civilized society, the body still responds exactly the same way with the identical "fight or flight" response. The stress sets off that same alarm in the brain, and the brain causes the same hormones to be released to sharpen the senses, to increase the pulse and blood pressure, to raise blood-sugar levels and redistribute blood flow, to deepen respiration, and to tense the muscles.

The further bad news is that, unlike our prehistoric ancestors who may have encountered a saber-toothed tiger once in a lifetime, we keep running into the modern equivalents of that tiger in a variety of forms over and over and over again—day after day, week after week, year after year. And every time our bodies respond identically, and that response is not only no longer useful, it is potentially damaging—even deadly! In short, as a species we are biologically overreacting to our environment!

The human body can deal with short-lived or infrequent episodes of stress and the body's autonomic response to it. But when stressful situations continue, the body is kept in a near-constant state of activation that increases the rate of wear and tear on our biological systems. Remember the analogy of a jet preparing for flight? How long would a jet plane last if it spent significant periods of its useful life in "readying for takeoff" mode rather than in simply being airborne?

In the past twenty years, many studies have looked at the relationship between stress and a variety of ailments. Even without reading the studies, it cannot escape you that when the stress response is repeatedly invoked, it can contribute to cardiovascular diseases such as hypertension and heart attacks, strokes, diabetes, ulcers, musculoskeletal disorders (such as neck, shoulder, or low-back pain), and other diseases.

And that is just the *physiological* side of the danger of stress. There is another important side to the effects of stress that is harder to measure using statistical analysis, but it is no less painful in terms of human suffering.

None of us is "better" under the pressure of stress. We become short-tempered, cranky, argumentative, unreasonable, and even unfriendly. In the worst of cases, we reject the love, care, and support of the people who care the most about us. We socially isolate ourselves, and this serves only to increase the pressure on us, since social support is a powerful stress-buster. I'll bet you can identify more than one marriage or relationship that has been the casualty of one or both partners suffering under the burden of too much unrelieved stress.

Stress is killing us—millions of us every year—and destroying our most precious relationships, and most of us are doing exactly the same thing about it: absolutely nothing.

I can't guarantee that getting your life in balance will result in you having a stress-free life. What I can guarantee, however, is that if you do everything you can to live a balanced life which reflects what is truly important to you and which is designed to help you turn your dreams into reality, there will be at least one less stressor on you. As you might imagine, many people experience significant stress when the life they *want* and the life they *have* are at variance.

Having what you want in life—spending your time and attention with and on the people and activities that *really* matter to you—is the best way I know of to relieve some of the stress we are faced with day after day and to return to our natural state of balance.

2

The Four Myths of Life Balance

> *Errors, like straws, upon the surface flow;*
> *He who would search for pearls must dive below.*
> ◆ JOHN DRYDEN

SOME OF THE FIRST THINGS that often need to be overcome when seeking to engage a higher degree of balance in one's life are the all-too-commonly-held myths and misconceptions about Life Balance and how to achieve it. The purpose of this chapter is to assist you to navigate through and around those myths. Here are four of the most prevalent ones in our society.

MYTH NO. 1: LIFE BALANCE IS ACTUALLY ACHIEVABLE

For many years I have taught courses involving Life Balance in a variety of settings such as universities, corporations, not-for-profit organizations, government agencies, and public seminars. You may find it interesting to know that one of the very first things I tell people is that *it is impossible to actually achieve Life Balance!* What I mean is that Life

Balance is not achievable as most people tend to think of it. My sense is that we most often imagine Life Balance as a state of static equilibrium in which things do not change. In this magic state of stasis, there are just enough of each of life's activities to make almost anyone happy. There is no stress. We have achieved Nirvana.

In the cold light of reason and experience, however, it must become clear to every one of us that in a constantly changing world our individual sense of balance—our personal Life Balance equation—will have to be constantly changing as well. There is no way that we can possibly find an answer—*the* answer—and tether ourselves to it for life with the expectation that it will keep us perennially happy. Our lives move much too fast for that.

Why, then, a book on the subject of achieving Life Balance if it cannot actually be achieved? The answer lies in the knowledge that there is much to be gained from the act of simply seeking Life Balance and that a fabulous harvest can still be reaped by striving after the goal even knowing that the goal cannot actually be reached. Consider that by seeking and moving toward a more balanced life you will achieve results and receive benefits that will make life better for you and for those around you *regardless of whether or not you reach the ultimate goal of achieving perfect Life Balance.*

But how do you effectively chase after a goal that is constantly moving, changing shape, and re-creating itself? The answer is that you must use methods that are themselves constantly moving, changing, and being re-created and that will result in you being able to constantly move, change, and re-create yourself. That is exactly what the tools and techniques in this book are designed to do.

The point is that you should not delude yourself into thinking that at some point you will have learned everything you need to know about Life Balance and that you will go on to achieve it and leave the struggle behind. Living life in at least some semblance of balance is a process that requires constant vigilance and action.

MYTH NO. 2: THE REAL ISSUE IS WORK/LIFE BALANCE

You may be asking, "Isn't this really just about realizing that I'm working too much?" Well, maybe and maybe not. It is certainly possible that you are working too much because many people are, but then again, the amount of time and attention you are already spending on your job may be perfect *for you*. It is even possible that you might want to increase the amount of time you spend in work-related activities in the future.

It is not the purpose of this book to tell you what you should be doing with your life—that's entirely up to you. What is your choice with respect to your work? Lots of people are able to work nearly around the clock, and they do it with a sense of fulfillment because it is their choice to do so. We might even say that they have achieved balance in their lives, because their lives reflect what is important to them and they have chosen to do those things that are important. When we meet these people, we are often surprised to discover that they seem to get energized from their seemingly overzealous work schedule rather than having it drain them. This is the case because they love what they do, and they have made it their choice to do as much of it as they can. They are, in a sense, being fed by their work.

If, however, you are finding that your life seems to revolve around your job at the expense of the rest of your life, it is likely that you are yet another victim of the myth of the work/life–balance dichotomy. Let me explain.

Everywhere there are books, magazine articles, seminars, tapes, and radio and television talk shows discussing the issue of "work/life balance." The mental image this creates for each of us is one in which your work is over "here" and the rest of your life is over "there," and your responsibility is to work out the conflict if there is any—and there usually is. A standard representation of this dichotomy is the traditional balance with a beam, a fulcrum, and a dish suspended from each arm on either side of the fulcrum such as that carried by Justice in most statues depicting her. This "either/or" mind-set forces us to believe we much choose between our work and the rest of our lives. Couple that frame of reference with the fact that most people absolutely must work in this day and age, and the results are clear: work comes *first*, and do your best with whatever time is left over. For most of us that construct leaves us with the uncomfortable but accurate feeling that the bulk of our lives *definitely* resides on the work side of the scale. Rarely is there any "balance" involved.

I don't like to think in terms of a work/life–balance dichotomy, and I do not talk about Life Balance in that construct. The truth is that our lives are *totalities* which require a mind-set that takes into account a high degree of integration, and this integration includes all the things that are necessary and important to us in our lives.

For years the image I have used to represent Life Balance is that of a circus bear attempting to hold his equilibrium on a flat circular platform, and that platform itself is balanced on a large ball. The circular platform is divided into slices of varying sizes like a pie, with each slice representing some element of your life. You are the bear.

We are never totally in balance, i.e., the platform is never fully at rest and parallel with the ground. Instead, life is a constant effort to keep the platform reasonably level. At the same time, for one reason or another, that platform will always be tipping down, first toward one edge of the circular platform, then another, then another.

We all know those times. Something happens that tilts our lives in one direction or another: we get promoted or we lose our position, a child is born or a parent becomes incapacitated, we begin training for a special sporting event such as a marathon or a long bicycle ride or we get the leading role in a community-theater production, we get divorced or we get married. The list is infinite because the list is made up of all the events that make up our lives.

We can almost feel our lives physically tilt toward dealing with these events—notice that there is no judgment as to whether such events are good or bad; they simply *are*—and it is appropriate that we do deal with them because these events are often pivotal and not to be ignored. Indeed, they *are* life. When these events hit, it tends to throw us off balance, and it is our responsibility to keep our lives reasonably balanced—if not immediately, then at least over time.

The point is that this is not a battle between time for work and time for the rest of your life, although to the extent that you hold this construct in your mind, that is exactly what it will be. Instead, the Life Balance wars of the twenty-first century are about prioritizing what things and what people are important to you and ensuring that you create ample opportunities for yourself to accomplish those things and to be with those people—while everything and everyone is crying out for your attention and time, some more urgently than others.

Achieving Life Balance in this environment isn't easy, and it certainly isn't simply a case of throwing a few more weights on the non-work side of a two-armed scale. It will help you tremendously in your efforts to achieve Life Balance if you stop thinking about it that way.

MYTH NO. 3: ONCE YOU'VE GOT IT, YOU'VE GOT IT

We'd all like to think that one day we will suddenly get clear about what exactly is missing from our lives, put it in place, and that will be that. You know how the fairy tales end, "And they lived happily ever after..."

Nice idea, but that is simply not going to happen. If it could happen, I would spend a few hours consulting with people, assist them in finding out what they need to add to their lives that is presently missing, print up a schedule for them to live by, and that would be the end of it other than the "And they lived happily ever after." I could probably charge a lot for producing those schedules!

Your Life Balance equation is unique to you and to your personal situation. Remember the bear on the circular platform? Well, at any given moment the pie-slice segments on the platforms of every person on the planet are different. Additionally, not only will what's on each of the segments change, but the size of each segment relative to the other segments will be constantly changing as well. Your circular platform, my circus-bear friend, is a personal—no, a *uniquely* personal—thing.

For example, right now the major issues in my life that make up the segments of my own circular platform look something like this: finish this book and get it to my publisher, train for the Hawaii marathon this winter, continue to develop new business for my company, re-design the corporate Web site, work closely with my wife to prepare for my daughter's entry into public high school in a few weeks, find a new place for my octogenarian aunt to live, support my dad in his present health challenges, and continue to handle a few garden re-design projects. The most important words in that previous sentence are "right now," because that list would have looked entirely different several months ago and much of it will look significantly different in just a few more months: the book will be finished and delivered, the marathon will be over, the Web-site re-design will be completed, my daughter should be several months into her high school career, my aunt will likely be relocated to a better living situation, and my dad will experience a full recovery. It is likely, however, that I will still be looking to create new business for the company and still be dealing with the garden, which seems to be one of those never-ending projects! I have no doubt that new activities will instantaneously present themselves to fill the void of those that have disappeared. Indeed, at this moment I could take an educated guess at what some of those will be and I would likely be fairly accurate. Then, of course, there are the bombshells that show up once in a while!

The point is that there is no single answer for Life Balance. There is no one-size-fits-all solution for everyone. There is not even a single answer for you. Think about it. What does your circular platform look like today? What would your platform have looked like six months ago? How about a year ago?

If you can, think back to what you were doing and where and with whom you were spending a large amount of time and attention ten years ago. Perhaps you were in a different job. Perhaps you were still in school. Perhaps you were single then and married now or married then and on your own now. Whatever your circumstances, just take a minute and remember what your daily life looked like. Now, imagine moving that life just as it was—each and every one of those activities—to the present day and visualize yourself dealing with it all now. If you can't imagine that very easily, you are not alone.

We change. Our life situations change. The issues in our lives change. And the Life Balance equation we create—consciously or unconsciously— needs to reflect that constantly changing internal and external environment. Indeed, what one needs to do to maintain a semblance of Life Balance over the course of an entire lifetime will change—not just from year to year, but if you are consciously applying yourself to the process, probably from month to month or even from one day to the next.

One of the key purposes of this book is to assist you to understand that you must frequently review your life situation and make conscious choices about how you are using your time. Doing that will cause you to automatically create a Life Balance equation that is reflective of the changes in you and the changes in the circumstances of your life.

Myth No. 4: I have to put others first

There seems to be a general belief in our society—and in many cultures which I have experienced—that we can genuinely serve others only when we put their interests ahead of our own. This concept seems to make logical sense in the far recesses of our hearts and minds, but it wilts when brought out into the sunlight and examined.

It is a rare person indeed who has not experienced the stresses of having conflicting desires—generally his or hers and those of another or of a group of people who are important in the scheme of things in that person's life. Earlier in our lives, we may have had parents who wanted us to follow a certain career path while our heart told us that our happiness lay in another direction altogether. We may have wives or husbands or partners or children or parents and other relatives who are pulling at our proverbial apron strings with their own agendas, desires, and needs. In the workplace, we face an unending set of demands from our employers, our managers, our peers, and our staffs—not to mention customers, vendors, and any relevant government regulatory agencies. Friends, acquaintances, and pets make demands on our time. Even the inanimate possessions we collect in life—houses, furniture, gardens, cars, bank accounts, investment portfolios, and just about everything else we have accumulated—vie for our attention.

Somehow many of us have it wired that it is only after we have met the expectations of others that we are to be permitted to make some effort to fulfill our own, very personal inner longings. Living this way is living from the "outside in" instead of from the "inside out," and it is what I call living in outer-centered reality instead of in inner-centered reality.[1] If you really think about this approach as the blueprint for living your life, however, you will begin to see that what you will construct is a life of disappointment and little or no fulfillment for yourself. You will also never experience anything even remotely like a balanced life, as your Life Balance equation is constantly thrown off by the demands of the people around you.

Look at it this way: There are three possible ways to live a life based on other people's expectations and demands. One is to allow other people to set your life agenda. There are many people who do this. You probably know some of them. They don't seem to have a life of their own; indeed, their lives seem to be reflections of the lives of the people around them in the sense that their very reason for existence appears to be tied to other people's wants, dreams, and desires. This may be fine, particularly if it is the truth of your heart. I will not deny that there are people whose only goals in life are to contribute to the dreams of others or to relieve hardship and suffering wherever it is found. That contribution, in fact, becomes internalized as their own dream. These people appear all over the world in a variety of settings and go about these duties joyfully. As pointed out earlier, they are energized and nurtured by these activities.

The problem arises, however, when one of us who is not naturally an Albert Schweitzer or a Mother Teresa performs the same seemingly unselfish tasks not out of choice but because we believe we *have to*. For these people, the mantra is often, "Well, if I don't do it, no one will," or words to that effect. The result of this approach is often resentment that burns quietly but hot beneath the surface of these people's helpful demeanors.

Some people attempt a second way, which at first blush may seem like a more moderate path and the best solution. What this looks like in this context is to not necessarily be responsive to *everyone* who makes demands on you but, rather, to be responsive—and totally responsive—to a small, close group of consciously or unconsciously selected people whose interests you feel you must protect at all costs. While membership in this group could change over time, it will frequently include close relatives such as parents, life partners, and children, a small number of "best" friends, and, unfortunately perhaps, almost everyone with any power over us.

This approach can work for some time. To be more precise, it works until what you are asked to do by a member of your small, close-knit group goes so much against the grain of what you really want for yourself that you are no longer willing to sacrifice what you want. Indeed, frequently you are no longer even willing to compromise, and you find yourself—largely as a result of years and even decades of suppressed resentment—snapping over to the third approach and often doing so with a malicious vengeance.

This third way is to insist that you come first, and that means carefully checking in with your self—your Inner or Authentic Self—to determine what is, in fact, important to you. From that discovery of your own dreams and desires, you then begin a lifelong process of using your time and attention to bring your dreams into reality.

Do not misinterpret what I am saying. I am *not* saying that you should not take care of others, but you should only do so if it is the truth of your heart. To do otherwise is to invite resentment. Interestingly, you will be surprised by how frequently what you really want to do turns out to be what other people want you to do anyway! Then, everyone is happy. But if you are living life at the other end of the range where you disregard your own urges in favor of other people's desires, you never get to ask yourself whether you are following your own heart because you are only responding to the demands of others.

All of us know of couples in which one partner or the other is suddenly seen as having "flipped out," leaving his or her life partner of twenty or more years, changing everything about his or her appearance, and transforming his or her lifestyle and living conditions until he or she is no longer recognizable as the same person. We generally throw these folks into some "midlife crisis" category and leave it at that. My feeling is that these people suddenly came face-to-face with the reality of their situations: They had been living their lives for others, and they are no longer willing to do so—for anyone! Time, they think, is running out, and they'd better get on the road to creating a little more of the life they want before it's too late. In such cases, the pendulum, as it were, seems to swing a little too much in the opposite direction.

The truth is that you will have to make a choice between pleasing all the people in your life—or at least some of the people in your life all of the time—and having a life that you find fulfilling and that you can make efforts to move toward one of balance.

The choice, as always, is yours.

3

A Few Fundamentals

THERE ARE A FEW FUNDAMENTALS involving Life Balance that are likely to affect your attempts to get your life more into balance. I prefer to see what's coming or likely to come or, at the very least, to have the ability to recognize something for what it is when it has fallen on me, and it is in this spirit that I offer the following fundamentals. In the area of Life Balance, just as in so many other things, forewarned is forearmed.

THE GREAT CONSPIRACY

Creating even a rudimentary sense of Life Balance is an uphill struggle. It may seem at times as though the great forces of the entire universe—including the people in your life—are aligned in some concerted effort to oppose your attempts to bring balance into your life. When you experience this, it is not your imagination!

In a certain sense, there is an unspoken conspiracy against you getting your life in balance. This conspiracy does not spring from some malevolent intention on the part of the people in your life. Indeed, there is undoubtedly no conscious awareness to thwart your attempts to become more balanced on the parts of your family, friends, and co-workers.

It simply is the way that it is. You will discover this soon enough if you don't already know what I mean. Your attempts to develop a discipline of daily meditation will be confounded by new demands on your seemingly only available time for such an activity. Your commitment to leave the office at a reasonable hour a few days each week and spend more time with your family in the evenings will be attacked by a rash of new work-related problems from which you can imagine no escape. A decision to begin a regular exercise program will be frustrated by sudden and unexpected inclement weather or your body serving up a new ration of aches, pains, and even illness. The kids will become more demanding or your spouse or partner will suddenly need more attention or seem to "go off the deep end." The possible manifestations of this phenomenon go on and on, but the manifestations are real. If allowed to do so, they can yield a mortal blow to your attempts to regain control of your Life Balance equation. Indeed, most often, this is exactly what happens to our good intentions—the seeming conspiracy rears its ugly head in one manner or another, and we immediately fall off the wagon.

In short, life will continue with all of its vicissitudes and accidents of fortune, but these need not necessarily derail your efforts to have a life more in balance and more to your liking.

First of all, do not despair! Remember, as I indicated earlier in chapter 2, that there is much to be gained from simply making the attempt to achieve Life Balance. Secondly, there is a purpose to everything, and it is possible to hold that the purpose of the great conspiracy is to test your commitment to the choices that you make along the way. In other words, the conspiracy can serve to strengthen your resolve.

When you stick to your commitment even in the face of a full frontal assault by the unwitting accomplices of the great conspiracy, making whatever adjustment may be necessary so that you can complete your plan of action regarding creating a new habit, as frequently as not the forces arrayed against you will dissipate. Time and time again, I have seen this to be the case.

THE LAW OF MIND ACTION

The Law of Mind Action declares that "things held in mind create after their own kind." In other words, whatever you are focusing your attention on is what you will get more of in life.

There are at least two possible explanations for this phenomenon. The first is that nothing has really changed in the absolute, but because of what you are "holding in your mind," your awareness of things and events that are the same as, similar to, or that mirror those held-in-mind images is heightened so they now stand out from the landscape into which they normally recede. For example, if you close your eyes for a few moments and, while they are closed, think of some color and then concentrate on it, you will see that all the items which are of that color in the room around you will "pop" when you open your eyes. You will see even the most insignificant splashes of that color stand out—a title on a book amongst hundreds on your bookshelves, a single design element in a complex drapery fabric, or a single bloom in a garden filled with flowers of all hues outside your window. All these things you would never have seen had that color not been "held" in your mind. Go ahead, try it.

The other explanation, which resides at the metaphysical end of the scale of experience, is that what develops around us in our world is actually created by the thoughts we hold in our minds. The Buddha says, "We are what we think. All that we are arises with our thoughts. With our thoughts, we make the world."

It doesn't matter to which theory you subscribe, because the effect on you is the same in either case. That is because whether you think that the Law of Mind Action is only causing you to *perceive* things differently or whether you believe that it is actually causing you to *create* things differently, you will react or respond only to what your senses tell you is the truth of the situation around you. By definition, that truth is determined by your subjective perception of the world around you and not by any objective reality, so you respond identically to the effects of the Law of Mind Action regardless of which is its actual underlying mechanism.

The Law of Mind Action is a powerful force in our universe and in our lives. Indeed, if metaphysicians throughout the millennia are to be believed, it is, in fact, *the* most powerful force in our lives. The problem with it, if there is one, is that people are generally unaware of it or its impact and then find themselves surprised when their worst fears come to fruition as a direct result of their worry. I like to remind people that, in the context of the Law of Mind Action, worrying is the same thing as praying for what you do *not* want to have happen!

There's one other thing about the Law of Mind Action you need to know: You can't escape it. Whether you consciously participate or not, whether you make efforts to monitor your thoughts or not, whether you attempt to change any destructive thinking or not, the Law of Mind Action operates in your life at its full undiluted strength. Like the Law of Gravity here on planet Earth, there is no escape from it nor is there the possibility of a "time out." What you think every moment of every day of your life—and whether these thoughts are conscious or unconscious is irrelevant—directly affects your experience of life. The American writer James Lane Allen articulated it exactly when he said, "You are today where your thoughts have brought you; you will be tomorrow where your thoughts take you. You cannot escape the results of your thoughts."

How this applies in the realm of Life Balance may be obvious to you, but it bears some mention here. When we want to use the Law of Mind Action to assist us in creating a more balanced life—much as we might use gravity to help us move something down a steep hill—it is imperative that we keep our attention on what *is* working, i.e., where we are getting the results we want and not on where we are not getting results. This is not a natural thing for us to do. If you are anything like me, you will find that your attention naturally goes to those elements of some plan that are not working, even when the overwhelming majority of the elements *are* working. For example, if we commit to doing something every day for a week and we actually do it every day but one, our attention will somehow attach itself to the fact that we "failed" that one time and not to the fact that we succeeded the other six times.

The antidote is to forcibly focus our attention on the things that are working and to consciously celebrate those. Because of the Law of

Mind Action, focusing on the positive results will, in turn, create more positive results. In *Heal Thyself*, White Eagle says, "When you concentrate upon negative things you give them life, but if you cease to think about them you withdraw life from them and they gradually die."[1]

Such is the case with the stumbles and the falls you may experience while traveling your path to greater Life Balance.

THE IMPORTANCE OF FOCUS

Human beings cannot multitask in the sense of focusing on more than one thing at one time. I know we all run into people in every walk of life who think they can do more than one thing at a time. Indeed, by this definition we may even think we ourselves can multitask, but the truth is that the thinking centers of the human brain have the ability to focus on one thing—and only one thing—at a time. We simply cannot be focused in more than one direction at once, and generally our attempts to do so result in "incompletes" in both areas.

What we have successfully learned to do is to create the *illusion* of multitasking, switching back and forth very quickly from one thing to the other—say, driving a vehicle while participating in a cellular telephone conversation. The human mind is able to handle momentary lapses in concentration, but we are not very good at doing two things simultaneously that use the same sensory organs for any extended period. We learn to do this switching-of-concentration trick so well that the transition is invisible even to us, and we are left with the illusion that we are doing both tasks equally effectively and simultaneously. The problem, of course, comes at the point when you truly do need to be fully focused on both things simultaneously, such as when the telephone conversation takes an unexpected and unwelcomed turn which draws all your attention at the very same time that a road emergency requires your full attention to your defensive driving skills.

To succeed, you will need to *focus* on whatever it is you are trying to change in your Life Balance equation. This will not be easy. If a great conspiracy attack doesn't completely derail you, it will at least make you try to multitask by focusing on more than one thing at a time. Don't do that! You will find yourself not having effectively dealt with either the derailing problem or your efforts to change. At times like this you will need to make a choice, and I cannot tell you what your choice should be, because that depends entirely on the circumstances and on you.

Notice that I am not saying it is imperative that you choose your commitment to Life Balance, although it's clear that consistently choosing something which conflicts with a more suitable Life Balance equation will not change your life for the better. What I am saying is that a commitment to Life Balance will require you to focus on what you are trying to achieve in a way that you might not now be used to doing.

About your workplace

Despite my warnings in chapter 2 against treating your Life Balance issues as a "work" versus "the rest of your life" dichotomy, it is likely that you will still find yourself struggling with your job as a major source of imbalance in your life. Indeed, at this juncture you may not be able to see clearly past the work/life–balance dichotomy itself—false as it is and damaging to the creation of a more desirable Life Balance equation as it might be.

If this is so for you, it is likely due to two contrary assumptions that we somehow simultaneously hold on to about the workplace. One is that we must do whatever is asked of us in the context of our employment no matter how onerous it might be. The second opposing assumption is that our employers—and most particularly, our personal managers or supervisors—are looking out for our best interests.

Neither of these assumptions has any basis in reality. That is not to say that your workplace in general or your boss in particular is executing some Machiavellian scheme against you. There is, in fact, nothing devious or conniving about either of these situations; indeed, the former is simply a function of our own beliefs about the workplace—beliefs over which we have complete control—and the latter results from a combination of a misunderstanding about the role of our managers and the impact of one of the immutable laws of the workplace. This is simply another set of facts that needs to be taken into account when you are attempting to adjust your Life Balance equation.

Let's take a look at each of these assumptions in the context of Life Balance.

First, recognize that while it is true that you are paid by your employer to perform certain tasks and that those tasks are often without clear boundaries or end points, you must understand that any boundaries which are placed on your availability need to be put down by you. It is not in the nature of organizations to do so. In a certain sense the workplace is very much like a child dealing with his parents in that it is always pushing the boundaries with its employees. The rule in organizations is everywhere the same: The more you do, the more you will be given to do. I have discovered this to be a fact of work life in every organization of which I have been a part—government agencies, small companies, global corporations, the military, and not-for-profit organizations. It is even the case in volunteer groups, professional associations, and clubs. Every one of them operates on the same unspoken rule: The more anyone does for the organization, the more opportunities that individual will have to do even more for the organization.

What this means is that it is up to you to determine what is a fair and equitable amount of your time and attention to devote to your employer's activities and exactly where it starts to cross over the line to an unacceptably high percentage of your available time and attention resources. While your employer will not assist you in making this decision or help you to mark the boundary, I have discovered that employers and organizations are surprisingly willing to honor those boundaries once they are laid down. And don't worry, if your employer thinks that you have drawn boundaries unacceptably generous to yourself at the expense of the company, you'll be told without any hesitation whatsoever.

I know we'd each like to believe that our bosses have our best interests at heart, and to a certain extent, I'm sure that they do. There are a few things that need to be understood about your relationship with your boss, whoever he or she might be, that affect your attempts to balance your life vis-à-vis your relationship to your work. First, your boss's attention is "up the chain of command" and not "down the chain of command." For the most part, our managers are looking at *their* managers to see what they need to do or how to move to the next level in the organization. This is particularly true in hierarchical organizations, which most American corporations still tend to be. Generally, managers give their full attention to their direct reports only when there are problems in that individual's area that could negatively affect the impressions the supervisors of those managers might have of *them*. Usually, as employees, we are not interested in that kind of attention from our managers.

Secondly, managers are focused on results and assign work with that in mind. Many of us—particularly those of us who are good workers and can be counted on to produce results—know this well from experiences with well-meaning supervisors.

Picture this: Some important project comes into the department, and it is part of the boss's responsibilities to assign it to someone. Who does the boss give it to—the person who doesn't produce results or the one who can be counted on to get the results needed to make the boss look good? You know the answer to that one already. Shortly thereafter another important project arrives, and the boss goes through the same thinking process and usually makes the same decision—the person who got the first important project now gets the second as well.

If this has happened to you—and I'll bet it has—you've probably found yourself sputtering in your mind, "But, boss, what about the other people in the department? Besides, you already gave me one important project." Probably because of some of the other workplace dynamics discussed in this section into which you may have bought, you probably said nothing, which only exacerbates the problem, because here comes Important Project No. 3! And on and on it goes until you reach the point of resenting first your boss and then your job.

At best you are left wondering what is going on with your manager. "Doesn't he (or she) realize what he's already given me to do?" Well, frankly, no, he doesn't. Once work has been assigned to someone in the department, the assigned work is completely invisible to the manager, who will continue to assign work without regard to what work has already been assigned. If you are the right person for the new assignment—and frequently you will be—you will get it regardless of what is already on your plate. If you remain silent as so many people do, this pattern will wreak havoc and totally destroy any attempts on your part to create a better Life Balance equation.

When you couple this results-oriented approach with the inclination of organizations to give more to those who do most, it makes for a one-two punch that will leave you and a balanced life out for the count.

What do you do? Sorry, but again the responsibility falls to you, and you get to be a magician this time. Your only recourse is to make the "invisible" work already on your plate "reappear" for your manager. One approach I have found that works well is to seek some guidance from your manager on your priorities in light of additional important projects being dumped on you.

"John," you might say (if your manager's name is John), "as you know I'm already working on the Castleton project that is due tomorrow, the Huffington project that is due Thursday, and the Gonzales project that is due the following Monday. Did you want me to put those aside to work on this, or can this wait until after those are completed?" The point is that you use the opportunity to remind your manager of all the things you are already doing for him and give him the opportunity to reconsider, or in the alternative, to give you some guidance as to what the priorities actually are.

And here is where it can get a bit difficult. Time after time people have told me that their boss tells them to "just get it done!" If that is the situation, you basically have two options: One is to stand firm with regard to your boundaries and do what you can to appeal to your boss's rational mind, which might include coming up with some creative alternatives such as re-assigning to another employee some of the work that has been previously assigned to you, using resources such as temporary workers or underused employees from other departments, hiring new resources, and the like. The other option is to cave and do *whatever* it takes to complete anything your boss throws at you, and brace yourself for more because it will be coming. You might as well also stop reading this book because you haven't a snowball's chance in Hades of adjusting your Life Balance equation to something you will experience as fulfilling!

But before you do stop reading, however, know this: I have counseled dozens if not hundreds of people who felt that there was no way they could ever say no to their bosses, but based on my recommendation that they do so, they tried it nonetheless. In almost every situation these people came back and reported that they were very surprised by the reasonable responses from their managers when they saw the situations into which they had placed their employees. Indeed, many of the managers acknowledged that they felt the same things were happening to them, and they didn't like it either! In almost every instance the employee and the manager developed a plan that worked for the manager, the employee, and the organization.

Why, you might be asking, would your boss be willing to negotiate with you about your workload when your expectation is that he or she will simply tell you what to do and you will do it, no matter what? The short answer is that your employer doesn't know that you are quite so willing.

There is another invisible dynamic at play here that puts a great deal of power in your hands. While every one of us approaches any potential confrontation with our manager from *our* point of view, which includes the fear that we might lose our job over the issue, we don't seem to realize that our managers have to respond to those same issues when we bring them up in the context of *their* fear that if the situation is not resolved to our satisfaction, we will leave! That fear is heightened when the worker involved is one of the manager's best, which, as noted above, is often the case in these kinds of situations.

In the human resources industry, it is commonly accepted that the cost of replacing an employee is somewhere between one and five times the annual salary of that employee, depending on how critical the position is, how long it is vacant, and how many of the open position's responsibilities are taken over by other employees. That calculation does include the average three to six months that a replacement employee takes to be trained, but it does not include indirect costs such as the time involved for the human-resources department and the manager and others to conduct and complete the search, and it does not include any direct costs such as employment-placement-firm fees and reimbursed travel expenses for candidates.

As you might imagine, the cost of replacing an employee is not the whole story. Even if unhappy employees do not leave but remain with the company, they are less productive and likely to be absent more often than satisfied employees.

If you have managed others, you know the truth of these assertions. Clearly, you would be more concerned if one of your best employees were seeking opportunities elsewhere than you would be if you needed to work out an acceptable solution to a situation with an employee who has approached you with legitimate concerns about his or her workload and a request that something be done about it.

You may have much more power to negotiate than you think you do. Use it wisely!

AMBIGUITY TOLERANCE

As I said earlier in this book, there is no sure-fire plan that will work for everyone nor even one equation that will work for anyone to reach the ideal Life Balance. To get close at any given point in our lives is about as much as we can hope for.

Through most of your journey toward Life Balance, you may not have an accurate view of where you are going or how to get there. You will be trying things, some of which will work and some of which will not, and then you will try other things, again, some of which will achieve the results intended and some of which will fizzle. Ecologist Marston Bates reminds us, "Research is the process of going up alleys to see if they are blind."

You will need to have or develop a high tolerance for ambiguity. This means that you are willing to hang out with things being unclear and uncertain for as long as it takes for them to become clear and certain—if, indeed, they ever do.

I recently interviewed a young woman who was interested in changing her career and wanted a coach to assist her with the change. A mutual friend had referred her to me. We were discussing the possibility of entering into a coaching relationship. As we talked about what she wanted from such a relationship, it became clear to me that the only thing she had any certainty about was that she no longer wanted to be in the field she was in, which was financial services.

That would have been fine with me, as I saw part of my responsibility as the coach in the relationship to be assisting her in determining in which direction she wanted to take her career. That, however, was not going to be sufficient for her.

She had, I believe, a very low tolerance for ambiguity, and she was unwilling to move in the direction of changing her employment until and unless she knew exactly what the end game was going to be. She was unable to even consider taking a few steps, waiting to see what happened, and then making adjustments and new choices based on the results of those first steps. She would be willing to move forward only with an executable step-by-step plan in place that she intended to carry out in its entirety—A to Z, as it were. This was clearly an impossibility given her present state of exploration.

Life's paths, unfortunately, are just not like that, and frequently we must make the choice to step away from what we have when we are clear that it is not what we want, with the expectation—the *faith*, if you will—that the very act of stepping away will create the next thing. My experience is that it does, but there are never any assurances. Business legend Harold Geneen said, "Uncertainty will always be part of the taking charge process," and taking charge of your Life Balance equation will be no different.

There are likely to be many times on your path to a more fulfilling life that you will feel the need to leave something behind—perhaps something that has been a part of your life for a very long time—without knowing what, if anything, will replace it.

To do that you will need to have or need to develop a high tolerance for ambiguity.

LIFE BALANCE EQUATIONS ARE SYSTEMS

The present circumstances of your life result from the system of living that you have created, and that system includes your habits and your Life Balance equation, without regard to the state of its balance or imbalance. A system exists when making an adjustment to any part of it affects any other part or parts of the system or possibly every other part.

General Systems Theory is a difficult and inexact science that includes concepts such as chaos theory, probability, information theory, and mathematical modeling. It was first proposed in the 1940s by the biologist Ludwig von Bertalanffy. We've all heard the layman's explanation of General Systems Theory in the example that when a butterfly flaps its wings in North America it causes a typhoon in East Asia. A simpler, more to the point example exists in whatever Life Balance equation you have now and your attempts to transition to one you may perceive as being better.

Let's say that at present you are spending up to seventy hours each week either at the office or doing office-related work at home. After taking stock of the situation, you decide that this state of affairs is not contributing to the quality of life that you want, so you commit to working no more than fifty hours each week. What will happen to the other twenty hours you used to consume at the office or doing office work each week? These hours don't just disappear. You can't bank them somewhere and use them sometime in the future!

No, something else—or perhaps everything else—in your life is going to have to shift. Perhaps you will take up a new hobby, perhaps you will spend more quality time with your family, perhaps you'll spend even more time being a couch potato or sleeping. What you do with the reclaimed time doesn't matter for the purpose of this example. The point is that you will be *forced* to do something with it. Your Life Balance equation is a system, and no part of it can be changed without affecting other parts of it. If instead of reducing the time you spend at work you were to begin something new, you would have to take the time from something else you are doing in order to engage in that new pursuit. In the system that is your Life Balance equation, everything is connected.

General Systems Theory is why you will take the changes to your Life Balance equation in incremental steps, changing only one thing at a time and seeing how the ripples from that one change affect the rest of the system before making additional changes.

Earlier in this book I pointed out that you will need to be in this for the long haul—mostly likely for the rest of your life. There are no quick fixes here. Further, there are no permanent fixes, either. What you decide is appropriate for your Life Balance equation today will not work for you tomorrow.

That, too, is part of the system.

SPACECRAFT AS A METAPHOR

Maintaining Life Balance is not unlike traveling by spacecraft. The in-flight operations of a spacecraft require navigation, guidance, and control. While these terms have very specific meanings in aerospace usage, they are also applicable to our attempts at changing our Life Balance equations.

In aerospace, navigation refers to the process of determining where a rocket is along its trajectory and where it will be later along that same trajectory if the trajectory remains unchanged. Guidance refers to the determination of the direction that a rocket needs to travel in order to reach a particular destination, and it is accomplished by computing the rocket's anticipated end position compared to the desired end position and using the differences to determine what changes should be made in the rocket's current direction to result in a smaller differential. Control is the process by which the flight path of the rocket is changed during its flight based on the navigation and guidance computations.

Rocket flight plans are not based on determining a specific course at the beginning of the journey and then maintaining it. Instead, they depend on knowing when the vehicle is *off-course* and making frequent course corrections. During the flight of a rocket, it can be off-course a significant amount of the time that it is in flight. After each correction by the control system, the rocket is back on-course only momentarily until it goes slightly off-course again, at which point the control module makes another course correction. The rocket keeps moving toward its destination only by ability of the navigation, guidance, and control systems to recognize each error and make what is usually an exaggerated course correction.

Your attempts to steer a steady course toward Life Balance will be very much the same. You will most likely be off-course to some degree most of the time, but with a reasonable amount of monitoring you can arrive with some accuracy at your predetermined destination.

The key elements of such a strategy are understanding and committing to the long haul and not losing heart when you find that you are off-course. When that happens, make like a rocket—make a course correction and just keep firing your jets!

4

The Importance of Support

How can one beam alone support a house?

◆ CHINESE PROVERB

AT ONE POINT IN MY CAREER I worked in a large high-technology company where I found myself at the center of a maelstrom of conflicting management styles in one of the departments where I was a senior staff member. Jack, the vice president in charge of the department, had a no-nonsense, directive—even confrontational—style. He was viewed by the majority of his staff as a micromanager in the extreme and completely insensitive to the people who worked in the department—particularly those who reported directly to him, although many others in the department also complained of painful interactions with the boss. Sadly, there was more than sufficient evidence to support these views.

After several years of this kind of treatment and several unsuccessful attempts by the senior staff to have Jack address the issues in some meaningful way, resentment and even anger had built to the point that several individuals complained directly to the CEO about their treatment by Jack, and some departing managers made a point of letting the CEO know that they were leaving the company largely as a result of their inability to work with Jack. As a result, the CEO determined that intervention from an outside management consultant was appropriate, and Jack and the entire senior staff began undergoing a series of diagnostic tools and participating in a succession of off-site meetings with the consultant in an effort to resolve the issues.

I was in an interesting position in that, due to unique circumstances, I had two very different relationships with Jack. First, I was a member of his staff and bristled under the same inconsiderate behavior and micromanagement that was affecting the rest of his direct reports. Additionally, however, I was into long-distance running, which was Jack's other passion besides the company. Since we lived in the same neighborhood we had taken to running together on occasion. Jack was a different person on those runs than he was at the office, and I think he leveled more with me about his thoughts and feelings during those runs than he ever had with anyone at work.

I discovered on our runs during this period that Jack was making a serious and sincere effort to change the way he was operating at work. We talked about what he was doing and what he might do differently in the future. What I saw at the office in the context of our conversations was significant evidence that Jack was, indeed, making monumental efforts to change his behavior and the relationships he had with his staff members. I don't believe the man could have tried harder to change. I fully expected that things would work out for everyone.

Surprisingly, however, they didn't!

What I saw happening at the office was hard to believe at first. I could see that Jack was changing—had changed. It was reflected in his tone at staff meetings, in the types of questions he asked, and in the manner in which he requested follow-up or gave out additional assignments. Bizarrely, his staff members seemed to be responding to Jack as though absolutely nothing had changed, and things continued much on the same track they had been on before Jack's transformation—and this was generally downward. On several occasions I even attempted to talk to some of my peers in an effort to have them see that Jack really was changing and that we should make every effort to support him in succeeding. They simply wouldn't or couldn't believe me.

It was all in vain. In the end, Jack was only able to change his relationship with his staff gradually as the members of his staff were replaced. Most moved to other positions on their own volition, their distaste for Jack's perceived management style having driven them to seek employment in other departments or even outside the company.

At the time, those results seemed puzzling, but as I thought more about it, I realized that not only was the whole situation *not* surprising, but it should have been anticipated.

Over time I've come to understand that relationships are systems, and as such they are subject to systems thinking and systems dynamics. Moreover, we ourselves are the ones who create and maintain those systems. For the most part, we have little inducement to change a relational system already in place.

Here is one way to think about the concept of relationships as systems. In our relationships with others—family, friends, housemates, neighbors, co-workers, and so on—each of us is like a unique puzzle piece. As we move into relationship with another person, together we "negotiate" the shape of the border between our respective puzzle pieces to something that will work for both of us. We may adjust the shape of our puzzle piece a bit; they may adjust theirs a bit.

At some point a subconscious arrangement is made in which each party understands how his puzzle piece fits into the other. This "negotiation" takes place using many parameters, including conversation, observation, interaction, past experience, and reputation. The resulting border may not be optimal for either or both parties because to some extent it will take into account such elements as the underlying basis for the relationship itself, the actual or perceived power level of each individual, and personal traits and idiosyncrasies such as each individual's degree of confidence, self-image, and level of self-esteem. For example, I may submit myself to a puzzle-piece-border relationship with my manager that allows him to yell at me "because he's the boss" when I would not allow such a situation as part of the border relationship with anyone else in my life. As I said earlier, these are compromised positions that are rarely optimal for either party.

We do this to some extent with everyone in our lives. You can begin to think of yourself as the central puzzle piece in a *system* of such relationship models, each of which has been subconsciously negotiated with you so the other person knows the parameters of how to respond to you and you understand how to respond to the other person. The longer any relationship is in existence the more concrete the border between the puzzle pieces becomes.

The truth is that we *train* others to respond to our behaviors in a particular way. We do this with others, and others do this with us, because first, it's easy, and second, for the most part, it works. It allows us to keep some degree of consistency in our relationships with others that permits us to keep life and its necessary projects moving forward with a minimum of disruption.

Problems occur, however, when one member of any relationship—Jack, for example—decides to make substantive changes in his or her behavior. The people whose puzzle pieces border on those of the person who wishes to change his behavior simply won't allow it! In the world of interpersonal relationships, this is tantamount to removing a central piece from a completed picture puzzle and attempting to replace it with a differently shaped piece. It won't work! Indeed, from the perspectives of those puzzle pieces bordering on the now-missing piece, the removed piece is still there! The shape of the missing piece is now defined by the pieces that bordered on it.

What happens is that we get stuck in our pictures of how someone is—indeed, how that person has actually trained us to think about him or her—and we continue to respond to him or her as though there have been no changes. In other words, Jack's staff members could not see the new Jack because the old Jack filled all the spaces in their experiential memories. They were all reacting to the pictures in their heads that they carried about Old Jack and not responding to New Jack as he was in real time.

This is yet another example of the power of the truth stated by Mary Baker Eddy in her nineteenth-century classic, *Science and Mind and Key to the Scriptures*, "The mind sees what it believes and then believes what it sees."

After some time, the lesson I gathered from the situation with Jack and his staff was very clear: If you don't get people to support you in changing, they will support you in being the same!

There needs to be an open renegotiation of the borders. This will result in the people around you supporting you with your intention to change rather than resisting your attempts to change and subconsciously undermining you because they are continuing to see you as you were rather than as you now are. Since we train the people around us to respond to us in particular ways based on how we are, it's really up to us to retrain them when we want or need to change how we are being.

You will be much more successful at making core-level life changes if you enlist the support of the people around you—those whose puzzle pieces border on yours in the variety of arenas that make up your life. It is difficult to attempt this alone, and it would be foolish to try.

People won't intentionally get in your way, but human nature is human nature, and most people have difficulty recognizing on their own that someone is making a concerted effort to change. Indeed, my experience is they don't remember even when I make a point to tell them, and I'm forced to remind them: "Remember? This is how it is now."

Very frequently our response to the present is a function of our experiences of the past. Past experiences can be so strong and have made such an impression on us—perhaps merely by consistent repetition—that it completely overwhelms anything contrary to its "truth" that may be happening in the present.

If you want to avoid the situation that Jack found himself dealing with, it will be necessary for you to discover those people who are *rely-*

ing on you not to change and then enroll them in the change you want to make. It will take repeated communication—probably a good deal of it.

You will have to think your way through this initially. Consider one arena of your life—say, work—and think about your puzzle piece in relation to those of the others in your workplace with whom you have significant interaction: your manager, peers, staff, customers, vendors, and so on. How have you trained those people to respond to you in the past? What will you need to communicate to each one to give you the best opportunity to effect a change in each relationship? Recognize that there may be as many individual communications necessary as there are people whose puzzle pieces border on yours. Do this for every arena in which you intend to change your behavior. You might consider creating a written matrix in each arena showing each person's name in one column, some words that describe the relationship you have now with this person in the second column, and the words that describe the relationship you want to create in the third column. Going through this written exercise is also likely to suggest a plan of action for communication with each person, which will grease the wheels for relational change.

We have our habits, you see, and then others build their own habits in dealing with us to some major degree dependent on ours. We cannot change our habits without disrupting the status quo, and people will resist such a disruption by the easiest mechanism available, which is usually denial. In these situations, denial often means not seeing that anything different has occurred and continuing with life just as it was.

There is also an important side benefit to discussing your proposed changes with other people in your life: accountability. I am a big believer in being held accountable by others. It's amazing how much I can accomplish when I know that someone is going to ask me if I did what I said I was going to do.

For example, as I'm writing this, it's very late—past midnight. I've been at my desk since sometime early this morning—before six o'clock—and it would be quite easy for me to go to bed, particularly since I have an early start and a fairly full schedule tomorrow. However, I told Kim, who has been my focus partner for several years, that I would finish this chapter today, and so that's what I'm doing. She is going to ask me about it first thing the day after tomorrow when we talk next because that's what we do for each other. In fact, that is the main purpose of our relationship as focus partners. And so, I'm pushing through and getting this assignment finished—something I might not have done if I were accountable only to myself for doing it.

In much the same way, the people in your life who would have naturally resisted your attempts to change can instead be enrolled to assist you in achieving your goal to change. Tell them what habitual behavior you want to change and what you want to change it to and then give them permission to call you on it when you are doing something other than what you said you want to be doing. You can even give them the exact words to use that will signal to you that they are doing exactly what you have asked them to do.

By bringing those around you into roles that support your intended change, you eliminate the possibility that they will become obstacles to your success. Rather, you make them part of the process which will ensure that you succeed.

5

The Habit Cycles

> *Habits are safer than rules; you don't have to watch them.*
> *And you don't have to keep them either. They keep you.*
> ◆ FRANK CRANE

UNDERSTANDABLY, WE HUMAN BEINGS prefer to think of ourselves as creatures exercising free will in every action and interaction as we go through life. Indeed, we believe that free will is ours by Divine Right, and we bristle at the suggestion that we undertake anything without the exercise of that prerogative.

Our day-to-day activities for the most part, though, are the result of unconscious habit and not the conscious exercise of moment-by-moment free will. This is not to say that we do not have the capacity to operate in free will at any given moment, but the truth is that we generally do not do so.

Rather, we do things consistently—and unconsciously—day in and day out without thinking and certainly without consciously considering what the long-term results of our actions are likely to be.

Consequences, however, do result from every action that we take, and too often, particularly in the realm of Life Balance, the long-term consequences of the habitual actions that we take on a daily basis would have been clear had we stopped to consider them. But we don't.

I am specifically thinking of a significant number of executives with whom I have worked who were truly shocked to discover one day that their spouses had "unexpectedly" left them or that their children were "suddenly" estranged or that their health was "without warning" all but beyond recovery. On reflection these people could all identify the points along the way where their words or actions could have predicted the outcome, but they simply hadn't been paying attention.

In truth, the paths that lead to these and similar tragedies are cobbled together by us over years and decades. The cobblestones we use are the individual actions we take on a daily basis, and too frequently, those actions are dictated by our personal habits. More than anything, our habits define us. They define our characters, our values, and ultimately, our lives.

The nineteenth-century author Charles Reade said, "Sow an act and you reap a habit. Sow a habit and you reap a character. Sow a character and you reap a destiny." Your destiny is subject to the actions you are taking today—this very minute—and those actions are more often than not the result of your system of habits.

It is important to understand that, while most of us relegate the general concept of "habit" to the "negative" or "bad" side of the ledger in our lives, habits have no intrinsic value in and of themselves. To be sure, there are bad habits that we can and all too often do develop, such as smoking or excessive drinking or any of hundreds more you can think of on your own. And just as surely, there are *good* habits that can be planted and nurtured, such as tithing or practicing wanton acts of kindness to strangers or, again, as many hundreds as you can think of on your own. Both of these extremes exist in the realm and range of habits, but they say little about habits in general.

Consider for a moment a habit as a thing separate from its potential negative or positive aspects—the bad or the good. The definition of *habit* that I'd like you to contemplate for this application is "a behavior pattern acquired by frequent repetition or developed as a physiological function and showing itself in regularity; an acquired or developed mode of behavior or function that has become nearly or completely involuntary."[1] Consider the possibility that the development of a habit can be a *practice*—a practical tool you can actually use to your advantage.

Each one of us is subject to what I call the Existing Habit Cycle. This cycle operates independently of whether a habit is "good" or "bad." At the same time that the Existing Habit Cycle causes us to react in accordance with our existing habits, that very reaction, in turn, reinforces the habit itself, which makes the next reaction all the more predictable. Figure 5.1 shows a depiction of the Existing Habit Cycle.

The Existing Habit Cycle works this way: Let's suppose you already have a particular habit—such as taking a walk with your partner or spouse immediately after dinner. When dinner is completed (the *stimulus*), you will experience a feeling of some urgency to ready yourself for your walk. In a situation where your habit has existed for some time, you may even experience this urging as almost uncontrollable. Indeed, you may start feeling significant mental, emotional, and even

HABIT

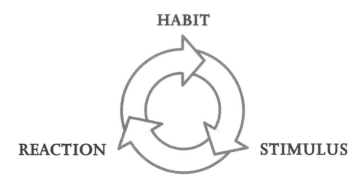

REACTION   **STIMULUS**

Figure 5.1. The Existing Habit Cycle

physical discomfort if you seriously attempt to resist the impulse or are somehow thwarted in your attempt to take your walk.

Note, too, that the stimulus can be completely separate and distinct from the underlying *cause* for the development of the habit. In our after-dinner-walk example, the underlying cause for the development of the habit could have been any number of things: a desire to lose weight, a need to walk the dog, a desire to spend some time communicating with your partner or spouse, and so on. But it is the stimulus—finishing dinner—and not the initial cause for the development of the habit that activates the reaction in the form of the walk actually taking place.

Think of one of the habits that you know you have—again, it makes no difference whether you or others consider it "good" or "bad." What is the nature of the habit? What is the reason the habit was developed, if you can remember or determine that? What stimulates the habit, i.e., what causes you to want to engage in the activity or set of activities that you consider to be the actual habit?

When operating in the Existing Habit Cycle, we respond to a given stimulus with a preordained activity or set of activities (the *reaction*). The reaction is inextricably connected to the stimulus like the two sides of the same coin. In our example, where a walk after dinner is an ingrained habit, it is likely you will take your walk when the stimulus of having finished your dinner triggers you to do so. Such reactions are frequently unconscious; that is to say, they are performed with little or no self-awareness. They have become, as it were, *automatic*.

Each time the same reaction is linked with a given stimulus, it creates a greater probability that future instances of the stimulus will result in the same reaction. Remember that consistent reinforcement ultimately creates an involuntary mode of behavior. The habit is reinforced and the cycle continues, driving the existing habit further into the unconscious and thereby making it more involuntary. In terms of our example, without some conscious interference on your part to change your well-developed habit, it can be accurately predicted that in the future finishing your dinner will result in an after-dinner walk.

We would probably all agree that an after-dinner walk is a good habit to develop for most people. Notice, however, that the dynamics of the Existing Habit Cycle do not change if we modify the reaction to the stimulus of completing dinner from a walk to something that most of us would agree is not a good habit, such as smoking a cigarette or moving directly into "couch potato" status by reclining on the sofa in front of the television for the balance of the evening. The system works identically in any set of circumstances and for any given habit—good or bad.

And this is the way most of us live our lives. We travel our paths through life doing activities that we would like to believe result from free will but that, instead, actually spring from well-developed and usually unconsciously created habits.

Think about just a few things in your own life for a moment. Don't you have certain things you do—rituals, if you will—peppered throughout your day—*every* day? Perhaps the day doesn't go right if something interrupts that first cup of coffee in the morning. Perhaps you are in the habit of meditating each morning. Perhaps you need a smoke break at certain times during the day or require a beer or cocktail upon arriving home before you can "relax." And about that trip home: Don't you find yourself taking the same route *to* work consistently and the same route *from* work consistently, even if the "to work" route and the "from work" route are not the same? These are all examples of habitual behaviors—involuntary in the sense that we don't consciously think about them before moving into action.

The point is that we all have our habits, and more to the point, to a greater extent than any of us realize or perhaps wish to realize, those habits create the quality of the lives we are living. Again, some habits can contribute positively to the quality of our lives, while some habits can do serious or even catastrophic damage to the quality of our lives. But habits they are, each and every one of them.

If you are going to change your own personal equation for Life Balance—consciously perhaps for the first time and then continually for the rest of your life—you will need to recognize your habits, determine whether each one is contributing positively to your Life Balance equation, and learn what exactly you can do about changing those that are not contributing to the life you want.

That's where the Habit Creation Cycle comes into play. The Habit Creation Cycle is the first step in a two-step progression you can use to turn the unconscious power that your habits have *over* you and your life into conscious power and then ultimately into unconscious power that works *for* you to create the life you want. The second step of the two-step progression is easy: At some point, you simply let the Existing Habit Cycle take over again because the new habit is ingrained in your behavior.

Figure 5.2 depicts the Habit Creation Cycle. The Habit Creation Cycle is a variation of the Existing Habit Cycle, but its power comes from the insertion of a unique dynamic: *awareness.*

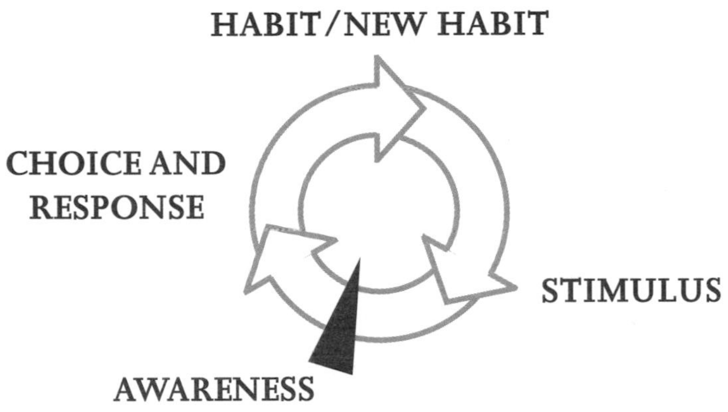

HABIT/NEW HABIT

CHOICE AND RESPONSE

STIMULUS

AWARENESS

Figure 5.2. The Habit Creation Cycle

Just as with the Existing Habit Cycle, the Habit Creation Cycle assumes that a habit exists which would normally cause you to react to a given stimulus with a preordained activity or set of activities. As discussed above, the repetition of that reaction in the Existing Habit Cycle causes the habit to become more ingrained. However, the introduction of a wedge between the stimulus and the reaction in the Habit Creation

Cycle disrupts the natural flow of the cycle and has the potential to significantly change the outcome. That wedge is awareness.

By remaining aware—mindful—of our habitual reaction to a given stimulus, we have the opportunity to change the outcome rather than simply moving automatically into reaction mode. In this arena, mindfulness means understanding what the stimulus is and what our normal reaction would be, coupled with an understanding of the likely results of that automatic reaction. It is further fueled by a desire to change the outcome for ourselves and for those around us.

At the point in the cycle when you would have normally just automatically "reacted," you now have access to something you weren't using before: *choice*. Choice is a powerful catalyst in that it has the ability to change everything about a situation from how you feel about it to the results that are ultimately achieved.

One result of accessing choice is that we tend to negotiate our way through life more effectively. Remember that a prerequisite to "choice" is awareness, and when we look at life's situations and the various options available to us from a state of awareness, we bring to the mix the full panoply of creative gifts we have available to us, including our intuition. Such creativity is noticeably absent from the automatic reaction model of the Existing Habit Cycle. In short, when in awareness, we make better choices.

The other interesting thing about being in choice is that there is no such thing as a *wrong* choice! The choice you make in any situation is simply, well, your choice. If you don't like the results that a particular choice creates in your future, then the next time you have the opportunity, simply choose something different.

The importance of choice in the Habit Creation Cycle cannot be overstated. It is, in fact, the key element that distinguishes it from the Existing Habit Cycle; it is, indeed, what transforms an Existing Habit Cycle *into* a Habit Creation Cycle. When we move into awareness and ultimately into choice in the Habit Creation Cycle, we have the ability to change an unconscious *reaction* into a conscious *response*—and, with respect to habitual behavior that you want to alter, this is where the rubber meets the road and where magic can happen.

Let's track an example. Let's say you are in the habit of settling onto the sofa as soon as you come home from work, where you watch television and then fall asleep until you are woken up to go to bed. While there is nothing intrinsically bad about this, you look at the consequences of this habit on your life and decide that you don't like what you find: you suffer from low energy, you weigh more than is optimal, and you are not sleeping well when you do finally go to bed. You make a decision that you will start doing something else—working around the house or garden, exercising, or some other active pastime—which is a logical solution to changing the situation.

The next evening, just as you walk through the door from work— the stimulus—you immediately feel the urge to head for the sofa in accordance with your Existing Habit Cycle. Instead, your heightened state of awareness—due, no doubt, to your decision on the previous day—reminds you that today you are to start making a choice: you can choose to head for the sofa as always or you can choose to do something more active. From this vantage point you can see the future: if you choose the sofa, it's more of the same or worse—a future of listless, sleepless obesity; if you choose something active, you just might change everything about that future.

That choice will present itself every evening from that time forward. Some days, you will choose to be active as your response. Some days you may choose the sofa as your response. If you choose activity and start choosing it consistently, the repetitiveness of doing that will not only prevent reinforcement of the original habit, but it will actually *create* a new habit replacing the old one of heading for the sofa. By consistently choosing activity over the sofa, at some point—most experts agree that the time period for the creation of a new habit is from four weeks to three months—your involuntary reaction to the home-from-work stimulus will be to *want* to be active. You have, in the words of the definition, developed "a behavior pattern acquired by frequent repetition." In fact, you will find that you have forgotten about the sofa—because you now have a new and more desirable existing habit.

At this point you can let the Existing Habit Cycle take over and keep you on track automatically. Your habit, as Frank Crane says, will now keep you.

Let me give you an example from my own experience of how it is possible to move from the Existing Habit Cycle into the Habit Creation Cycle and, ultimately, back into the Existing Habit Cycle, and by doing so, change or eliminate a habit that is not supportive of the results you want in your life or of your quality of life.

For the first half of my life I was a relentless nail biter. The condition of my fingernails was an embarrassment through my childhood, in high school, in university, and on into graduate school. Nothing I tried—and believe me, I tried just about everything—had worked.

The weirdest part about this habit was that I had not one iota of awareness about biting my nails—indeed, I had no recollection of ever doing it—but the evidence on the tips of my fingers was indisputable. Either I was biting my own fingernails or someone else was doing it for me without my knowing it. Through the application of basic logic I was able to quickly eliminate the latter possibility. In terms of my behavior, the Existing Habit Cycle was totally on automatic and in full swing.

By the time I was in my late twenties, I was seeing my situation as potentially career limiting. Self-consciousness about the state of my fingernails began to erode the optimistic self-confidence I had felt most of my life. This was becoming a major problem!

While I certainly didn't call the various elements of my habit by the labels I am using today, it became clear to me that I had to figure out what the stimulus was that caused me to unconsciously go into nail-biting mode and then figure out how to either stop the stimulus from occurring or prevent myself from reacting to it with my habitual involuntary reaction.

All it took was for me to start the process of looking for the stimulus. While I had successfully learned to manage my behavior in front of others so that I did not bite my nails in business meetings or when with friends, I more than made up for that "down time" by gnawing on my fingernails almost nonstop while driving! I don't think I was a particularly nervous driver; indeed, I did and still do count myself amongst those who genuinely enjoy driving. No, I had simply arranged my habit so that its stimulus was an activity I generally did alone, thereby eliminating at least some of the embarrassment.

Notice that this is one of those examples where the stimulus was separate and distinct from the underlying cause for the habit—whatever the cause was. If I had been biting my nails as a direct reaction to some anxiety about driving, then the cause and the stimulus would have been the same. That, however, was not the case. In truth, I never learned what the underlying cause for my nail biting was, and frankly, it didn't matter. I was interested only in the impact the habit was having on the quality of my life—not good!—and in what I could do to change the habit to something better. Understanding why I was biting my fingernails didn't seem like it was going to assist me in achieving those results. As Werner Erhard used to say, "In life, understanding is the booby prize."

Clearly, I needed to do one of two things: either stop episodes of the stimulus from occurring or prevent my reaction. Stopping the stimulus wasn't an option—I was having a hard time imagining myself explaining to others that I didn't drive because it caused me to bite my fingernails! No, the answer lay in preventing the reaction.

I started wearing gloves. The choice, every time I got into my car, was whether or not I was going to put on those gloves. When on some occasions I decided, for whatever reasons, not to wear the gloves, the result was that I ended up chewing down one or more of my fingernails. Every time it happened, I decided I would make a different choice next time. Sometimes I did, sometimes I didn't.

Ultimately, I got to the place where I wore the gloves without fail whenever I was driving. I wore gloves on long journeys and for short trips to the supermarket. I wore gloves for my daily commute to and from work. I wore gloves in the worst of the heat of California's summers. I took gloves along on business trips and wore them when driving rental cars. I developed a "no exceptions" policy to wearing gloves when driving.

It got to the point that wearing gloves became essential to my comfort in driving, much as wearing a seatbelt had become years earlier. I had developed a new habit—wearing gloves while driving—and that new habit precluded my ability to engage in my old habit—nail biting while driving.

As an amusing aside, I always thought I must have looked ridiculous driving around in a 1978 MG Midget wearing driving gloves, but I didn't care. I was getting the result I wanted, and that's all that mattered. Interestingly, my wife, whom I met during this period, later told me that one of the things which really attracted her to me was that, when I picked her up for our first date one August night, I was wearing driving gloves. She thought I looked elegant!

It took some time, but the Existing Habit Cycle around my fingernail-biting habit finally ceased to exist, and I was able to begin driving without gloves and without running the risk of biting my fingernails. I haven't worn driving gloves in over twenty years—and my hands look great!

Think about one of your own habits—one that you would like to change because it is not giving you the results you want in some area of your life. Analyze the habit. When do you do it? What event or activity is the stimulus? If you know why you do it, that information might be helpful, but as indicated in my own example, the "why" of a habit is less important than understanding the stimulus and the reaction that constitute the habit itself. Next, develop a quick mental plan to change either the stimulus or your reaction that would result in breaking the cycle. The less complicated, the better.

Changes you attempt to make through the use of Habit Creation Cycles could—and probably will—feel unnatural and forced at first. This is a natural and very common result. Let me explain.

A hierarchy in competence exists with respect to almost everything that we do or attempt to do. While it stands to reason that we feel more competent doing things we have practiced over some prolonged period of time, there are more refined aspects to the dynamics of competence that are worth some explanation.

I think you would agree that with nearly any subject, we have the ability to move from a place of some level of incompetence to some level of competence. At the same time that we elevate ourselves from incompetence to competence, we move from discomfort and self-consciousness to comfort and self-confidence about the skills involved. We do this in dozens, perhaps hundreds, of disciplines over the course of our lifetimes. For example, we begin life unable to read or write and gain competence. If you look back on your career, you moved from some level of incompetence with respect to the required duties of the job to your present level of competence.

This is also the case when we learn new habits—we move from some level of incompetence about a new habit to some level of competence, and there are levels of discomfort and self-consciousness involved in the learning process. The Competency Hierarchy is shown in figure 5.3.

There are four phases in the Competency Hierarchy, each with its own unique characteristics.

THE COMPETENCY HIERARCHY

UNCONSCIOUS COMPETENCE

CONSCIOUS COMPETENCE

CONSCIOUS INCOMPETENCE

UNCONSCIOUS INCOMPETENCE

Figure 5.3. The Competency Hierarchy

Phase 1. Unconscious incompetence occurs when you are not competent to do something and you don't even know what you don't know about it. For example, if you talk with a young child about driving you will soon understand that the child doesn't know the first thing about driving, although he might play at it and even be convinced that he could do it. To a child, driving looks like going fast, turning the steering wheel, and having fun. The child is *unconsciously* incompetent to drive—he doesn't even know what he doesn't know about driving.

Understand that unconscious incompetence is not a bad thing. Indeed, it is something each of us possesses about many of the disciplines and practices about which another may be very competent—and we have remained so through choice. As just a few examples of my own, let me point out that I consider myself unconsciously incompetent with respect to flying an airplane, fighting a forest fire, driving a big rig, bungee jumping, scuba diving, climbing Mount Everest, performing surgery, and smashing atoms—and the list could go on and on.

Phase 2. Conscious incompetence exists at the point at which you begin to discover what you don't know about a subject or practice. Frequently this occurs when we are still incompetent with respect to a new discipline but have undertaken to learn it. The sheer volume and mass of the material to be mastered is often overwhelming and can make us uncomfortable. Think about sitting behind the wheel of an automobile for the first time after obtaining your learner's permit. Driving is no longer about the images you may have held as a child. *Now* it's about pedals, shifting gears, street signs, other cars, crosswalks, parallel parking, and on and on. It is all suddenly so overwhelming!

The conscious incompetence phase is daunting and uncomfortable, but it does represent a higher state of awareness in that it is movement toward competence. Ask yourself, if you had to choose, who would you give your car to—someone who can't drive and thinks driving is all about going fast and steering around objects or someone who likewise isn't competent to drive but is painfully aware of all that it entails?

Phase 3. Conscious competence is that point at which we are competent to perform some task, but we feel the need for heightened awareness to ensure that we do what needs to be done. We have the competence but not necessarily any degree of self-confidence, so we are vigilant in substitute.

Remember, if you can, those first few weeks or months after you got your driver's license. If you were anything like me, when you got in the car you were much more aware of everything that needed your attention than you probably are now. For some time after we first get our licenses, we tend to check the placement of the mirrors, we do not attempt to do other tasks at the same time that we drive, and we otherwise give our full attention to the task of driving. This phase represents a significant improvement over the previous two phases simply by the fact that competence itself has been attained.

Phase 4. Unconscious competence is that stage in the hierarchy when we are fully competent at a task and we no longer need to think about what we are doing to remain competent; indeed, at this stage we no longer need to be mentally alert or even present to remain competent. Having reached this stage in my driving abilities, I can drive on an interstate highway, such as U.S. Route 5 to or from Los Angeles, pass a sign that reads something like "Bakersfield—89 miles," and in what seems like the very next instant, pass another sign indicating "Bakersfield—65 miles"! I bet you can relate. I was able to go unconscious in terms of driving for about twenty minutes while my car was hurtling down the highway at seventy miles per hour because my driving abilities have reached a level of *unconscious competence.*

Another way to think of unconscious competence is "habit," which is why this is relevant to the discussion at hand. When you have an ingrained habit—good or bad—you have developed it to the level of unconscious competence. You do it without having to think about it— it is, in the words of our definition from earlier in this chapter, an acquired mode of behavior that has become nearly or completely involuntary (read: "unconscious").

If the habit is one that is contributing to the quality of your life, unconscious competence is a good thing. If not, you will want to change it. But to change it you will have to take yourself back down the Competency Hierarchy to the level of conscious *in*competence, and as noted earlier, that is generally not a comfortable place to be. It can be overwhelming and can frequently lead to abandoning your attempts to change your habitual behavior.

Don't let it! If you can see the discomfort associated with moving back down the Competency Hierarchy as a natural part of the process of moving into the Habit Creation Cycle, you will be prepared for it when it happens. You might even learn to recognize that discomfort as a positive sign that you are progressing toward your goal, because you will be.

If all else fails, just remember how silly I must have looked—and how uncomfortable I truly felt—wearing gloves year-round in my little red sports car!

6

Your Life Balance Categories

THE LIFE YOU ARE LIVING right now *is* your Life Balance equation. At one extreme, you may be deliriously happy with that equation, and at the other extreme, you may feel the urge to chuck the whole thing and start over again. It is also possible that you are reasonably content with your Life Balance equation but that you want to adjust it a bit here and there.

Most people do not know where to start if they want to make changes. We tend to look at our lives as a totality, or particularly in times of stress, we compartmentalize our perception and look at only one or two areas—generally areas that are not working for us. I have discovered that if I am able to organize the various activities of my life into categories I am better able to understand the whole picture, discover trends, and note where I would like to make changes.

Sorting the activities of your life into a few suitable categories may seem initially daunting, so as part of my Life Balance workshops, I created and offer participants a "temporary" set of categories that can be used. These categories can then be employed to determine what one's present Life Balance equation looks like.

For convenience—and because it fits with my own lifestyle—I have divided the areas of my Life Balance equation into eight categories, which are listed below along with an explanation of what I mean by each. Please note that these categories are *completely* arbitrary, and you might decide to divide one of these into two or more parts, or to combine two or more into one, or to use a totally different set of categories. With time, you will discover the right set of categories for your own personal Life Balance equation, and that is the set you should use. If you know what that set is now, by all means use it. If you don't, consider using this set (or some variation of it) until your experience and intuition provide you with an alternative, more personal set. You might want to keep some notepaper handy while you read this chapter for the purpose of creating your own personalized list of Life Balance categories. You will be using either the set of categories listed below or a set you have created on your own in exercises later in this book. Personalizing the list to your own circumstances is optimal.

The eight categories I use (in alphabetical order) are

Community and Contribution. Whether we are consciously aware of it at all times or not, we live life in relationship with the rest of the people of Earth. Success and fulfillment in life are not only about what you do for yourself and your close circle of friends and family, but they are also about what you are doing to make the world—and you can define *world* to mean just about anything from your neighborhood to the entire planet—a better place for others. How are you contributing to the quality of others' lives? What are you doing to reduce suffering, to increase joy, to build bridges of understanding, to produce peace? My experience is that personal fulfillment comes in direct proportion to our service to others, particularly serving those who, for whatever reason, are unable to take care of themselves. Albert Schweitzer said, "I don't know what your destiny will be, but one thing I know: the only ones among you who will be really happy are those who have sought and found how to serve."

Community and Contribution activities can range from writing a check to a charity to helping at the local soup kitchen. They include things as varied as cleaning out your closets looking for items of clothing to donate, performing *pro bono* work in your chosen field, or volunteering as a Big Sister or a Big Brother or at the local hospital. Community and Contribution activities can be part of a formal program, such as coaching the Little League or tutoring children in math or reading through the local school system, or they can be completely informal and, indeed, solitary, such as visiting the elderly in retirement and nursing homes or spending time with a lonely neighbor. What are you doing to serve your community and to make a contribution?

Family and Friends. The eighteenth-century writer Samuel Johnson said, "If a man does not make new acquaintances as he advances through life, he will soon find himself left alone; one should keep his friendships in constant repair." This statement is certainly as true today as it was in Dr. Johnson's time. And in this modern age of familial diasporas where relatives are spread from one end of the nation— or even the world—to the other, his advice applies just as equally to family members.

And while the difficulties of maintaining relationships with "extended" family are understandable, many people are having difficulty working what has become known as "quality time" with their spouses, partners, and children into their lives, even when those people are living with them under the same roof. Family-oriented and parenting magazines are replete with articles on how to spend more quality time with your kids or your wife or your husband. It is almost as though we have forgotten how to just be with our loved ones. The inability to make time for meaningful interactions with family members, which will in turn nourish and strengthen those relationships, is a crisis of major proportions.

In this environment, it is necessary that we consciously strive to keep our relationships in "constant repair," as Dr. Johnson put it. The category Family and Friends is intended to include all those things you do to nourish your relationships with your family and friends— whomever it is you include on that list of people. Family visits; vacations taken jointly with distant family members; holiday get-togethers; regular phone calls, cards, letters; and now, in the Internet Age, the exchange of e-mail and .jpg photograph files are all appropriate activities to be included in the Family and Friends category.

Fun and Frolic. We have all gotten so serious! Stop and think for a minute. When was the last time you went out for the sole purpose of just having a good time? When was the last time that you allowed yourself to get silly? When was the last time you laughed so hard your stomach muscles hurt?

Too many people are finding that the first casualties of their hectic pace of life is their ability to have fun and their sense of humor. More people than ever are living the life described by Woody Allen when he said, "Most of the time I don't have much fun. The rest of the time I don't have any fun at all."

And yet the importance of including fun in our lives has been heralded for over 2,500 years. It was Herodotus who said, "If a man insisted always on being serious, and never allowed himself a bit of fun and relaxation, he would go mad or become unstable without knowing it." How many of us, I wonder, have gone mad without knowing it?

The purpose of the Fun and Frolic category is to give you awareness into what activities you are doing just for the sake of having fun. What activities you include in that, of course, are up to you. As in anything, what looks like the greatest fun to one person will look like a painful experience to another. The trick here is for you to be honest with yourself. If you do something—whatever it is—as a gift of relaxation to yourself, then it probably qualifies as a Fun and Frolic activity. If you do something because it is someone else's idea of fun and you go along for any number of reasons such as peer pressure, wanting to be with a particular person or group, or because "everyone from the office is expected to attend the company picnic," then, while it may qualify for one of the other categories (e.g., Family and Friends or Work and Career), it *isn't* Fun and Frolic. Fun and Frolic is about what you do for fun for *you*!

Health and Fitness. Recognized health authority Adelle Davis said, "As I see it, every day you do one of two things: build health or produce disease in yourself." By including activities into your life that fit into the Health and Fitness category, you are making an effort to build your Life Balance equation on the side of health and not disease.

Far too many people believe health and fitness to be simply the absence of aches, pains, and sickness. On the other hand, those who have successfully integrated health and fitness into their daily lives— made it an integral part of their Life Balance equations—know that there is a palpable presence to health and fitness that contributes to one's overall quality of life. Consider for a moment where your attention goes and how much your life changes when you are feeling ill; indeed, at such times we often feel like we have fallen into a hole and our only goal is to get out. But we can do better than that. By creating Life Balance equations which include activities that are likely to keep us healthy and fit, we build a solid structure on which our lives stand that makes it harder for disease to reach us.

The Health portion of the category includes getting sufficient rest, eating the right foods, and doing whatever else is appropriate to good health, including regular medical and dental examinations to keep your body in the best condition possible.

There are a myriad of Fitness activities at every possible level from which to choose. For some people a walk around the block three times a week will be all they are willing or able to manage. Others will not be content until they have broken the three-hour time requirement for entry to the Boston Marathon. There are hundreds of activities that you can do all by yourself, with one or two other people, or with a large group.

These include walking, hiking, swimming, cycling, in-line skating, ice-skating, running and jogging, skiing, weight lifting, Pilates, and yoga. There are competitive sports such as golf, tennis, handball, bowling, racquetball, and dozens of martial-arts disciplines. There are team sports such as basketball, baseball, football, soccer, rugby, hockey, and volley-ball. There are formal teams and "pick-up" games. There are serious players and those who just want to have some fun and fool around. There are professional coaches and fitness trainers and Monday-morning quarterbacks and games made up with last-minute rules. It is unlikely that you can think of a set of circumstances representing your ideal fitness activity which cannot be accommodated.

As the folks at Nike like to say, "Just do it!"

Money and Finances. If you have scanned ahead, you will have noticed that there is a separate category for Work and Career that has yet to be discussed. You may be asking yourself why, therefore, is there also a Money and Finances category? Aren't they the same? Well, no, they are not, although I do understand that many people think of them as one and the same thing. This is natural because, for most people, the vast majority of their income comes from their salaries or wages.

There is much to be said, however, for developing a worldview that permits you to think of your Work and Career and your Money and Finances as two separate categories. The benefits of this are many and include beginning to see your work as having the purpose of feeding your sense of personal fulfillment and not just your bank account. By developing a consciousness about your money and finances that is distinct from your beliefs about your job, you open the door to an inflow of prosperity that is based on something other than your ability to earn an income.

Even if you cannot get yourself detached from the concept that the sole source of your money supply is your job, there is still much to be gained from developing habitual activities that will protect, monitor, and grow your money once it has been received. Such activities could include budgeting, savings programs, investments, retirement planning, developing multiple streams of alternative income, and home refinancing—at the time I am writing this, home-mortgage rates are the lowest they have been in over forty years.

If you aren't paying attention to the state of your money and finances, you can bet that no one else is either!

Personal and/or Spiritual Growth. Allow me the presumption, if you will, that the kind of person who would pick up a book like this in the first place is someone who is interested in his or her own personal or spiritual growth. For many of us, this is the primary motivation that moves us along life's path, i.e., learning about ourselves and about how to express more of our Higher Selves in our daily lives.

Such a quest does not happen purely by accident. Marcel Proust said that we don't receive wisdom; we must discover it for ourselves after a journey that no one can take for us or spare us. That journey takes intention, and the mindful expressions of that intention are the activities that one undertakes to accelerate his or her own personal unfoldment. These activities stretch along an almost endless range of possibilities—classes, books, tapes, discussion groups, retreats, meditation, affiliation with church and spiritual groups, participation in the arts—whatever you know feeds your soul and brings more of your authentic self out into the world. These are the activities of the Personal and/or Spiritual Growth category.

What are you doing on a regular or a cyclical basis to ensure that you are moving your program of personal or spiritual growth forward?

Projects and Hobbies. Each of us enjoys certain activities that add texture and spice to our lives. The types of things that fall into the Projects and Hobbies category are as many and as diverse as the people who do them, such as singing in a choir, acting with a community-theater ensemble, collecting, boating, playing bridge, computer technology, gardening, reading, painting, playing a musical instrument, dance of any and all types, listening to music, athletic activities—the list is literally endless.

It is also fairly safe to assume that each of us will always have one or more of these projects or hobbies in our lives, so it makes sense to always include them in our Life Balance equations—or at least a space for them even though the nature of the activity might change. Playing piano has long been an important part of my life, and it is likely to remain so for the rest of my life. On the other hand, I am presently in the process of replacing the plantings in a corner of our garden, and while that project will likely take several months to complete, at some point it will be over and done with. What I know, however, is that as soon as the garden project is completed, some other project—possibly house-related, possibly not—will present itself for consideration and I can choose whether or not to take it on. If not that one, then I will certainly choose another one.

What are the things that make your heart sing? The activities that go into your Projects and Hobbies category can be lifelong pursuits or brand-new hobbies you want to try out for the first time. They can also be the preparation for and completion of a one-time event such as redecorating a room or planning a special event such as a birthday or anniversary party. It doesn't matter what the activity is, but as long as it is taking some portion of your time and attention, you will want to include it in your Life Balance equation.

Work and Career. Most of us find that a significant amount of our time and attention is involved in dealing with work and career issues. There are, however, two very distinct and differing approaches to the activities involved in work and career. Most people are at the *effect* of their work in that they find themselves reacting to what happens in their workplace. The general *modus operandi* in many organizations is crisis management—sometimes it's throughout the entire company, sometimes it's in only one or two departments, sometimes it's just the way an individual handles himself or herself. These people are also the ones who seem to fall into the work/life–dichotomy trap more often than others. To them, life is about carving out some time—however little it might be—when they will not be forced to deal with work-related issues. Frequently they do not succeed. Many have simply given up.

Then there are those who deal effectively with work and career emergencies when they arise but who also allot some portion of their time and attention to planning and developing their futures. Frequently these people have a healthier relationship with their work and career in that it has not completely taken over their lives or so infringed on every aspect of life that they must attempt to "steal" guilt-ridden time to do non-work-related activities.

No matter which approach is yours, it is a safe bet that you will have a significant portion of your Life Balance equation in the Work and Career category, and it is important to understand how these activities are affecting you and your attempt to balance your life.

I cannot stress enough that these eight categories are intended as a starting point only. You will notice that there are some activities which could fit into any of two or more of the categories. For example, if you are an avid golfer, depending on the circumstances you could decide that the time and attention you expend in playing golf belongs in the Health and Fitness, the Projects and Hobbies, or the Family and Friends categories or even in all three.

There is nothing wrong with having a single activity contribute to your Life Balance equation in several categories. For example, almost every year I either bicycle in one or more of the five- or six-hundred-mile rides or run in one of the marathons to raise money for the organizations that provide assistance to those living with HIV and AIDS. The months of training necessary to participate in these events contribute to the Community and Contribution, the Health and Fitness, and not surprisingly, the Family and Friends categories of my own personal Life Balance equation.

Nor is it necessary that you "cover" every category with some activity or set of activities. For example, it is certainly possible, although I would imagine rare, for someone to consciously choose to forgo any Fun and Frolic for some period of time. Or perhaps someone might have done well enough in the stock market or in Las Vegas that they no longer have any interest in Work and Career, at least in regard to it providing them a living. Although it would never be my own choice, I do know people for whom undertaking any activity in the Health and Fitness category would occur only in the rarest of circumstances.

Note also that two activities which look identical on the surface could be placed by you into two different categories depending on the underlying reason that each was undertaken. Take my writing, for example. When I write books such as this one or articles for business journals and even my own newsletter, the writing activity falls into the Work and Career category, but when I write verse for one of my poetry books, that same writing activity is now more properly categorized as a Projects and Hobbies activity.

Once you have determined which categories are right for you—or if you have decided to use temporarily the set described in this chapter—you are ready to see what insights the Life Balance Equation Process has to offer you.

7

The Life Balance
Equation Process

> *Though no one can go back and make a brand-new start,*
> *anyone can start from now and make a brand-new ending.*
>
> ◆ *ANONYMOUS*

IT IS THE THESIS OF THIS BOOK that no matter what your Life Balance equation is—and this chapter will help you discover it and, possibly, how you feel about it—you have the ability to change that equation to something which is more likely to provide you with the results you want to have in your life. This thesis, however, begins with the requirement that you know what your Life Balance equation actually is and where you stand with respect to its effectiveness for you and for your goals.

If you know where you want to go, you need to know where you *are* or you can't get there! If you were to call me up to ask directions to my house, the first and most important question I need answered before I give you any directions is this: From where will you be starting your journey?

I am a strong believer in the importance and power of process. As quality expert W. Edwards Deming said, "If you can't describe what you are doing as a process, you don't know what you're doing." The three-exercise process in this chapter is designed to, first, determine from what point you are starting your journey (*Your Present Life Balance Equation*) and then, second, where it is ideally you would like to go (*A Future Life Balance Equation*). The third and final exercise is the development of a set of steps (*Your Five-Step Plan for Better Life Balance*) to get you from one Life Balance equation to the other, similar to the set of directions I might give you to get you from your present location to my home if you were coming over for a visit.

Unlike our house-to-house directions analogy, however, you will not be attempting to make this journey all in a single step or even in a series of steps that have been determined up front and that are then simply executed. Remember that your Life Balance equation is a system, and as such, every time you make a change anywhere in the system, it affects something somewhere else in the system. It would be foolhardy to attempt to change everything at once—if it were even possible, which it is not.

Instead, this process is designed to allow you to make adjustments in your Life Balance equation in incremental steps. To ensure that you experience the full power of this approach, you will start with the *one* change that you believe will make the most difference in your Life Balance equation. The awareness and effort necessary to replace a "small" existing habit which is causing you some difficulty with a newly created habit are exactly the same as that necessary to replace a "large" existing habit which is causing you a great deal of difficulty. Consequently, we'll start with your largest existing and troublesome habit. The risk is no greater, and when you succeed, the returns are significantly higher.

Remember, too, that this is not a "one-time" thing. You are learning a cyclical process that you can use for the rest of your life. In subsequent cycles you will continue to hone your Life Balance equation and deal with areas and issues that do not make the first cut. As often as not, though, many of those lesser issues simply evaporate in the course of the changes you make to deal with the greater issues because of the systemic nature of a Life Balance equation.

At the same time, recognize that new issues involving your Life Balance equation will arise as either a direct or an indirect consequence of the solutions you will be implementing. It is likely that most of those issues you could not conceive of today. This is another reason that it is imperative for you to understand that you are learning a lifelong *process* and not simply participating in a one-time fix.

A few words about the ideal environment in which to practice this process are appropriate here. When you are working on this process— both now and in the future—set aside an hour or more in an environment that is quiet and in which you are not likely to be disturbed. Turn the telephone off and disable any other device that could "go off" and interrupt you. Do whatever is necessary to ensure that you can give this process your full physical, mental, emotional, and spiritual attention.

While it is not necessary that you complete the entire process without interruption or in one sitting, it is important that you complete each of the three exercises in one sitting and, preferably, without interruption.

OK, let's get started.

EXERCISE 1: YOUR PRESENT LIFE BALANCE EQUATION

In the first exercise of the Life Balance Equation Process, you will take a snapshot of what your Life Balance equation looks like right now. There are several ways to approach obtaining this snapshot, but the one that I have found to be the best involves simply getting a sense of where you are spending your time and attention rather than mathematically calculating what hours you are spending doing what.

The first thing you will need is a form for the graphic description of your present Life Balance equation. You can download the form from my Web site at *www.spiritemployed.com* in Adobe Reader (.pdf) format, or you can simply create your own. If you want to create your own, all you need is a piece of paper about eight inches square. Draw a large circle on the paper and mark the approximate center of the circle with a dot. Your form should look something like figure 7.1.

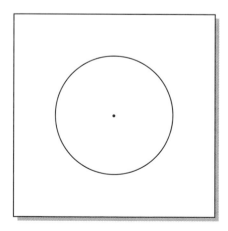

Figure 7.1. Life Balance Equation Form

Label your form "Present Life Balance Equation." Have a list of your Life Balance categories on a separate piece of paper handy nearby. This can be the list I suggested in chapter 6 or it can be a personalized list you have created yourself.

To begin this exercise, choose a time and place when you will not be disturbed for about thirty minutes, and begin by just sitting quietly for a few minutes. It will probably help for you to close your eyes, which will block out some of the distraction.

While you have your eyes closed, think first about yesterday. What did you do? Where were your attention and your time spent? Did you spend most of the day with family and friends? Was it a workday that required your full attention for almost the entire day on your job responsibilities? Just get a feeling for what the day held for you. Don't try to calculate how many hours you did what, just allow yourself to get the feeling of the day.

Then back up in your mind and do the same thing for the day before yesterday. On what and with whom did you spend your time and attention? Perhaps you had an appointment at the bank or with your lawyer or a mortgage broker. Maybe you left work early so that you could attend your son's recital or your daughter's volleyball game.

Then think back over the previous week. A few things of importance to you will likely stand out in your mind; make a mental note of those. You will begin to sense themes and perhaps see what I refer to as "ribbons of activities" that flow from one day or week to the next and that give your life a particular rhythm. Make a mental note of all such things that present themselves.

Think back over the previous month with the same eye toward getting a sense of where, with whom, and on what you have been spending your time and attention. Go back another month or two. Perhaps think back over another three months of your past and attempt to capture the sense and feeling of your life during that time frame.

Note that if you were on vacation or on a lengthy business trip, those periods will feel much different to you than your regular schedule will. If you like, isolate those periods in your mind, but consider including the activities they entailed in one or more of your Life Balance categories, particularly if they are recurring ones.

When you have completed reviewing your past for as far back as you are willing or able to go or for as far back as makes sense in your particular circumstances, open your eyes and immediately create a pie chart on your Present Life Balance Equation form. Look at each of the entries on your list of Life Balance categories and determine whether it was represented at all in the mental review of your last few months that you just completed. If it was, then assign it a "pie slice" more or less in proportion to the degree of its presence in your life over that period of time. If it was not present at all, just write the category in the white space outside the circle on your form. Go through your entire list and complete your pie chart with each slice of the pie representing one of the categories and its size representing how much of your time and attention was spent there over the period.

Remember the bear on the circular platform from chapter 2? To a certain extent what you are doing here is drawing the circular platform on which you have been balancing during the immediate past months of your life.

When completed, your form might look something like figure 7.2. When you have completed it, either turn it over or put it away so that

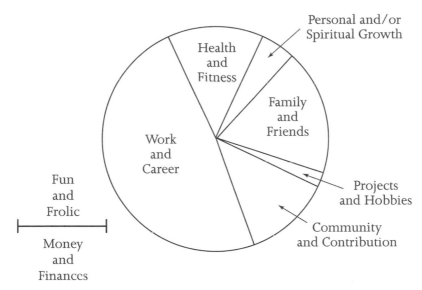

Figure 7.2. Present Life Balance Equation

it is not a distraction while you are completing the second exercise of the process.

I am frequently asked whether one should count sleep time. It doesn't really matter, so long as you either always count it or never count it. My personal preference is to not count it because most people will then find themselves blocking off somewhere between a quarter and a third or more of the circle to mark their sleep time depending on how long they sleep. My preferred approach is to monitor waking hours only.

There is no wrong way to do this exercise! It is an attempt to present you with the facts of where you are spending your time and attention and on what. What is most important is that you are honest with yourself and tell yourself the truth by writing down as accurately as possible what you discover while thinking back over your last several months. Remember: *Denial precludes transformation*, so if you decide to fudge the results of your personal investigation for whatever reason, you won't have the information you need to move your life in the direction you want.

What you will also need to do is to ensure that whatever method you use to create your Present Life Balance Equation is the same method you use for the next exercise, which is the creation of a Future Life Balance Equation. For example, if you are the type of person who leans more to a "count the hours" approach rather than a "it feels like this" approach, you will want to ensure that you do the same thing as you move into the next phase of this process. Otherwise, you will be comparing apples and oranges, and you won't get optimal results.

When you are ready, whether immediately or at some other time, move to the second exercise in the process.

EXERCISE 2: A FUTURE LIFE BALANCE EQUATION

From the first exercise in this process you will have completed a graphical representation of what your Life Balance equation has looked like over the past several months. That's important information, but it isn't enough to assist you in making choices *right now* that can help you create more of the life you want.

You cannot change the past. On the other hand, your future is wide open. You have the ability to create it any way you want. You can create a future that looks identical to your past—many people do—or, at the other extreme, you can create a future that looks nothing whatsoever like your past. Creating a future identical to your past takes no effort at all; indeed, it is what will happen automatically as a result of your habits. Creating a future that is different from your past, however, will only happen if you are clear about what you want that future to look like and if you are mindful of what you are doing and how this will either contribute to or detract from your ability to reach your goal. Habits unchanged will always re-create the past. That's where the second exercise of this process comes into play.

In this second exercise you will attempt to take a snapshot of what one of your possible futures might look like. At present there is no future in existence, so you will need to create one from your mind, set it as a goal, and then begin working toward it. This is the true power of this process.

You will need another form identical to figure 7.1. Label it "A Future Life Balance Equation." This title acknowledges that this graphic representation is merely one of an infinite number of future Life Balance equations you could create.

You will again need to have your list of Life Balance categories available beside you. Make sure this is the same list you used for the first exercise or you will have difficulty reconciling the results of the two exercises and then coming up with a plan in the third exercise in this process.

If you are doing this second exercise at a later sitting, again choose a time and place when you will not be disturbed for about thirty minutes, and again begin by sitting quietly for a few minutes with your eyes closed.

This time, while you have your eyes closed imagine yourself waking up in your bed on some morning in the future. Make it a bright and cheery day with sunshine streaming in through the windows.

You wake up in a wonderful mood. The day is full of expectation and you can't wait to get up and get the day's activities started. What is it that has you so excited? Ask yourself and wait for the answer. It will come.

And as you see yourself lying there in your bed on some future morning, imagine yourself thinking that life has, indeed, been *very* good lately. You are feeling centered, calm, relaxed, and not stressed in any way. You are excited about the days and weeks that are to come. You notice that your body and your spirit are thrilled with the activities that you will be engaging in during the upcoming weeks. What are they? Who will you be doing them with? Notice what things stand out in your mind and make a mental note of them. What are the themes of this future time? What are the ribbons of activities that flow forward from your then-present into your future and give your life rhythm? Make a mental note of anything along these lines that presents itself to you.

Pay particular attention to your emotions and feelings and to any sensations in your body as you sit in the present imagining this world of your future. How does this future feel to you as a possibility? Is it possible for you to just be with that future as a potential reality or do you have judgments about its viability or your ability to create it? Notice any beliefs you might have about this future and about your ability to make it a reality. Notice, too, how you feel about any judgments and beliefs you might have.

When you have a good sense of what activities will make up this bright future, start sorting them in your mind into your Life Balance categories. Again, be sure to use the same categories that you used for the first exercise—this is *extremely* important!

When you feel complete with this portion of the exercise, open your eyes and immediately create a new pie chart representing a potential future on the Future Life Balance Equation form. Again, assign "pie slice" sizes more or less in proportion to a category's importance in the future as you imagined it. And, just as in the first exercise, if a category simply was not present, write it in the white space outside the circle on your form. Go through your entire list and complete your future pie chart with each slice of the pie representing one of the categories.

The final part of this second exercise is to compare the two Life Balance equation forms that you have prepared. Take out the form you completed in the first exercise and place it next to the form you just completed in the second exercise. Take a look at both forms. What do you notice? Where are the differences? Where are the similarities? Give yourself at least five minutes or so to study first one and then the other of your completed forms and see what thoughts and ideas come to you. Listen carefully for intuitive messages.

Most people discover a significant disparity between what they are actually doing with their time and what their hearts tell them will make them happy and give them more of what they want from life. Many people are truly shocked by what they discover from this simple process. It would seem that many of us hide the truth about our Life Balance situations from ourselves. But that is consistent with the "surprise" element so many people experience when one or more parts of their lives start falling apart—marriages, relationships, health, finances—simply because they haven't been paying attention to what they have or haven't been doing in those areas. It's really not much of a mystery, but it is certainly surprising to many.

No matter how in or out of synch your two Life Balance equation charts happen to be, there is likely to be one major difference that will strike you right between the eyes. It may be the discovery that you are spending too much time and attention in one area of your life. Conversely, it may be that your comparison suggests that you are not spending enough time in some other category of your Life Balance equation which you think is important to your well-being. My experience is that most people have no trouble picking that one thing because it literally jumps off the pages at them.

Find yours, and when you have found it, you are ready to determine what kind of course correction you wish to make—just like a rocket's guidance system—except that your course correction, rather than a single burst from a jet engine, will be a complete step-by-step plan which will ensure that your intended change is effective. The development of that plan is the third exercise in this process.

EXERCISE 3: YOUR FIVE-STEP PLAN FOR BETTER LIFE BALANCE

Figure 7.3 shows the form for the Five-Step Plan for Better Life Balance. This is another form you can download in Adobe Reader (.pdf) format from my Web site at *www.spiritemployed.com*, or you can make up a form with a word processor or simply use plain paper. Just be sure to include all five steps of the plan because each one is integral to its successful completion.

Let's take a closer look at each of the steps of the Five-Step Plan at the same time that you complete it for yourself:

Step 1. Decide which *one* Life Balance category you are going to change and then describe the change you want to make. That change

Step 1. The change I want to make in my Life Balance equation:

Step 2. What I will do to effect this change:

Step 3. The items I will need to take care of:	**Step 4a.** Date complete:
1.	
2.	
3.	
4.	
5.	
6.	
7.	
8.	
9.	
10.	

Step 4b. My overall completion date:

Step 5. My support network for this change:

Figure 7.3. The Five-Step Plan for Better Life Balance

may be to increase the time and attention you are expending in a particular area or it might be to decrease the time and attention you are expending. An important element about step 1 is to state the nature of the change with some degree of particularity.

Remember, too, that your Life Balance equation is a system. Consequently, it is best to make changes in one area only and then let your daily life settle down before implementing any additional changes. That will eliminate or at least minimize any unpleasant surprises that could be caused by attempting to change too many things at once.

For example, let's say that what strikes you when you compare your two completed Life Balance equation forms is the fact that you don't seem to be doing enough in your Health and Fitness category, and you want to change that. You decide that what you want to do is to create the habit of regular exercise. For this example, you might write something like "I am going to get into a regular exercise routine" in the step 1 box of the Five-Step Plan form. Think of the step 1 written entry as the completion of the statement, "What I am going to do about this situation is..."

Complete step 1 of your Five-Step Plan.

Step 2. State specifically what you want to do to accomplish the change described in step 1. The best way to do this is to transport yourself in your mind to the future world you are going to create and then simply describe what you see around you. How are you acting? What different things are you doing? What things are you no longer doing that you notice are absent? Just describe that world.

In step 2, answer the question, "How are you going to accomplish the change you described in step 1?"

To continue with the example of increasing your time and attention to Health and Fitness, you might write something like "I am participating in a regular fitness and exercise program that includes at least one regular fitness class such as aerobics, bicycle spinning, or dancing, which meets at least twice each week. I also do additional fitness training or other exercise at least one other day each week." Be clear, concise, and measurable. You know when you've done it; you know when you haven't.

Now complete step 2 of your Five-Step Plan.

Step 3. Write down all of the items you will need to complete that are necessary to get you from where you are to where you want to be. Be sure to consider anticipated barriers. In step 3, answer the question, "What are all the individual items I will need to handle in order to accomplish what I planned to do in step 2?"

It is also important to understand that one of the key purposes of step 3 is to ensure that you don't fall into the trap so many of us do when we start out on the path of good intentions. That trap is not anticipating and planning for decision points and potential stumbling blocks and then, perhaps since we did not anticipate them, not even recognizing them when we come across them. That trap is one which I've fallen into myself more times than I really care to remember.

For instance, in a situation nearly identical to the example we are following here, at one point about a decade ago I found myself desperately in need of increasing my attention on Health and Fitness. I decided to join a fitness center, but a year later I still hadn't done so! When I looked back over that year, I discovered that I had consistently failed to make a pivotal decision without even realizing that I was failing to do so, and this unconscious failure prevented me from moving forward toward my goal.

The issue was simple enough. Was I going to join a gym near my home or a gym near my office, which was about forty-five minutes away? Every time I would focus on one of the options, all the reasons why it was not the better choice would be presented by the chattering monkeys in my mind, but then, when I focused on the other option, Monkey Mind would change its tune and I would soon be convinced that this really wasn't the better choice.[1] Since I was not particularly effective at managing Monkey Mind in those days, the result was that I just didn't deal with the decision at all, and as I said, an entire year went by and I was no closer to my goal. Once I discovered what had happened, I immediately committed to making a decision, and that decision resulted in my completing my plan in short order. The decision? Since in those days money was not an issue, I joined two fitness clubs—one near the office and one near my home!

The completion of step 3 of your Five-Step Plan can help prevent these problems. By thinking through and then writing down each of the individual items you will need to handle to get yourself from where you are to where you want to be, you will also have the opportunity to discover potentially derailing decisions, objections from others, and other issues that could prevent you from reaching your goal. By making it a requirement that you deal with the decision, the objection, or the issue as one of the items that you list in step 3, you eliminate the possibility that the decision, objection, or issue will surreptitiously throw you off your path to your objective without you even realizing it.

For example, if I were dealing with the same Health and Fitness issue today, my step 3 item entries might look something like this:

1. Choose a health club close to home or work and then join it.
2. Get a fitness evaluation to determine my fitness needs and goals.
3. Select a fitness class to join and join it.
4. Calendar my fitness time at least two months in advance.
5. Never cancel a fitness period because of an unavoidable demand in my schedule without rescheduling it within forty-eight hours.

Notice that at this point, I am not attempting to resolve the issue identified in item 1—I am only identifying it as something I know I will need to handle before I can move forward. That's really all it takes.

Now complete step 3 of your Five-Step Plan.

Step 4. One of the most important aspects of making changes to your future is to determine *when* that future is. Author Leonard Sweet said, "The future is not something we enter. The future is something we create." Part of that creation is the timing. In step 4 you determine completion dates for each item you listed in step 3, and from that information you calculate a final completion date for the entire Five-Step Plan.

The completion dates for the individual items in step 3 are listed in step 4a, and these generally are straightforward. If you don't know an exact date, just make one up. You can always adjust things later when you have more information as you travel farther down the road toward your objective.

By choosing an overall completion date for your Five-Step Plan (step 4b), you are basically answering the question, "When will I have converted this Five-Step Plan to a new habit or a set of new habits so that I can let the Existing Habit Cycle take over?" Obviously, the overall completion date identified in step 4b cannot predate any of the dates in step 4a. It is also important to remember that you do not want to choose a time frame for the execution and completion of your Five-Step Plan that will prevent your ability to create its activities as new habits using the Habit Creation Cycle. You may want to put the overall completion date out far enough so you will be sure that the Existing Habit Cycle can take over. That's the easiest and most sure road to successfully changing your Life Balance equation.

Recognize, too, that your overall completion date need not be a hard calendar date, such as April 10 of next year, although it certainly can be. Another way to choose an overall completion date is to cast yourself once again into your future in your mind's eye and look at your then immediate past to see what success will look like to you. This is basically the same process you used as part of the second exercise when you took a mental journey to your own future, experienced what it felt like to have a sense of great Life Balance, and then took a look around to see what activities had caused that feeling. What you would do this time is look back from the perspective of your future on your imaginary past and describe the condition that you would define as success at that point in time. For instance, in our Health and Fitness example, you might describe something like this: "I will be a member of a fitness club within twenty days, and within ninety days I will have attended that club regularly for at least eight weeks." In this example, you would know that "attended that club regularly" means the specific description you gave in step 2.

Now complete steps 4a and 4b of your Five-Step Plan.

Step 5. In chapter 4 we covered the importance of support. To reiterate, your chances of success in changing your life—or even one piece of it—through this process (or any other, for that matter) is almost nonexistent without the support of the people around you. Indeed, as the examples in chapter 4 showed, if you don't get the support of others for your intended change, the people around you will automatically support you remaining the same, and you don't need the process of changing your habits and behavior to be any harder than it already is.

In step 5 of your Five-Step Plan, you will determine who is in your support system for this specific change and ensure that you do what is necessary to get the support you need to be successful. A key part of that support system is yourself, so you should also use this opportunity to commit to succeeding with your Five-Step Plan.

Support can take a variety of different forms. It can be just sitting down with your family, friends, or co-workers to tell them how you are planning for things to be different in the future. It can have a very active element in that you ask someone to actually do something, such as join you in some activity, hold you accountable for what you say you will do, or make some other accommodation to your hoped-for changed circumstances.

Going back to our Health and Fitness example, the entry for step 5 might look something like this: "I will ask my friend George to partner with me either by joining the fitness club and attending the activities with me or by supporting me by my reporting to him my weekly success until this becomes a personal habit."

Note too that after determining what your support system is going to be and who is involved it may be necessary for you to go back to steps 3 and 4 to make some additions or adjustments.

Complete step 5 of your Five-Step Plan.

You have now completed a powerful tool useful in taking you into a new future you will create. Computer-design guru Alan Kay tells us that the best way to predict the future is to invent it, and through this process you are doing just that.

The next thing to do is to execute the plan. Develop a "no exceptions" policy to the implementation of your plan and you will be so successful in creating the changes you want in your life that other people will accuse you of performing miracles! Strict but gentle self-discipline is one of the foundations of success in this process.

A FEW FINAL THOUGHTS ON THE PROCESS

When you successfully complete your Five-Step Plan, it is not time to stop! After successfully completing your plan, you should redo all three exercises in the process no less than a month but no longer than three months after your overall completion date.

There are several reasons for this. For one, by that time the system represented by your then Life Balance equation will have reached a point of stasis, so it is a good idea to see what has happened to the relationships between all your Life Balance categories. Remember, adjusting any one of the Life Balance categories—which, after all, is the point of the Five-Step Plan—will cause others to shift also. In short, you need a new snapshot of your Life Balance equation, because the one you have from the point in time prior to the execution of your Five-Step

Plan is now hopelessly out of date and the information it contains is of little value to you.

The best thing to do is to go through the three exercises in this chapter again—and again and again—for the rest of your life if you want to get the maximum benefit from the process and as close to a balanced life as you can get, given the fact that achieving true balance is impossible.

Monitoring your Life Balance equation is an ongoing and a never-ending process. To experience its full power you will need to make reviewing your Life Balance equations and developing a Five-Step Plan to get from one to the other, well, a new habit. A good way to do that is to use the process every three to four months. If you use a calendaring system of any type—whether paper-based or electronic—one effective discipline is to schedule your planned Life Balance process reviews for the entire year in advance.

Remember that the state of your life is the natural result of the choices you have made or are continuing to make. If you want to change your life, it is necessary for you to change your choices, and you can only make true choices when you are living in a state of awareness or mindfulness.

Otherwise, it's all just habit → stimulus → reaction → same habit over and over.

PART II

Mastering Life Balance

8

The Balance Master's
Factorial System

bal•ance \'balǝn(t)s\ *vt* : to adjust or apportion to achieve proportion, harmony, or symmetry

mas•ter \'mastǝ(r)\ *n* : a person who possesses mastery (as of an art or technique)

fac•to•ri•al \fak'tōrēǝl\ *adj* : involving or based on replication with a variable introduced in each replicate

MOST PEOPLE COULD FAIRLY easily determine that the probability of selecting the ace of spades from a full deck of cards laid out face-down on a table would be one chance out of fifty-two, or $\frac{1}{52}$. What would be the probability of picking up as the very next card the king of spades from the remaining fifty-one cards? The correct answer is one chance in fifty-one, or $\frac{1}{51}$. The probability, then, of selecting first the ace of spades and then the king of spades as the first two cards from a full deck laid out face down would be the product of those two numbers ($\frac{1}{52} \times \frac{1}{51}$, or $\frac{1}{2,652}$).

Factorials are used in mathematics to calculate the probability of a series of possible events. As an example, consider the probability of selecting *all* the cards in exact descending order from a deck of cards placed facedown on a table. This would mean choosing the ace of spades first, then the king of spades, and so on descending through the remaining spades, then descending through all the hearts, the diamonds, and the clubs until only the two of clubs (the lowest-ranking card in the deck) is left. The probability of doing this is calculated by multiplying the probabilities of each separate event. The answer is the product of $\frac{1}{52} \times \frac{1}{51} \times \frac{1}{50} \times \frac{1}{49} \times \frac{1}{48}$ and so on down to $\frac{1}{1}$ after the final choice between the remaining three of clubs and the two of clubs has been made and only the two of clubs remains. (When only the two of clubs remains, the probability that you will pick it up last is 100 percent—one out of one, or $\frac{1}{1}$.)

When calculating the probability of actually completing this amazing feat, the numerator—the number above the line which represents the number of ways of doing this correctly—for the fraction that results from this series of multiplications remains "1." However, the denominator—the number below the line which represents the total number of combinations in which the cards can be selected—quickly becomes astronomical. And this is just as you would expect if you think about how difficult it would be to actually perform the feat of selecting the cards one at a time in precise descending order when they are facedown.

In mathematical circles, this type of multiplication is based on the number of possible permutations or combinations of different things (here, the number of different ways that a set of cards can be selected) and is known as a *factorial*. The factorial function is useful in various types of calculations and is most often used to calculate the probability of events. The power of a factorial comes from its repetition of multiplication with an identical variable in each of the repetitions. The traditional notation $n!$ represents a factorial for a positive integer. Given that $n! = n \times (n-1) \times (n-2) \times (n-3) \times \ldots \times 3 \times 2 \times 1$, in the case of our example of a set of cards, $52! = 52 \times 51 \times 50 \times 49 \times \ldots \times 3 \times 2 \times 1$.

The power of the Balance Master's Factorial is also based on repetition with a variable in each of the repetitions, although this is more by discovery than by design. As I have refined my ability to balance my own life over several decades and have sought ways to share with others what worked for me, I ultimately determined that a natural balance resulted by focusing on seven key areas during the course of a week. Interestingly, these areas were not to be treated equally in that each one did not need to be engaged every day. At one extreme, one activity requires daily attention, and at the other, one requires attention only once per week. The number of repetitions for the others were evenly spaced between those two boundaries.

Indeed, the more I learned about myself and the way that balance was present in my life when I paid attention to it—or fled when I didn't—the more I determined that there was a set pattern which I could use on a weekly basis to increase the probability that my daily activities would contribute to my Life Balance rather than denigrating or possibly destroying it.

The result is the Balance Master's Factorial, a system of gentle self-discipline that has allowed me to chart my progress against predetermined ideal patterns. These patterns both reflect and incorporate the Life Balance categories discussed in the first part of this book.

The Balance Master's Factorial is an easy-to-use precision methodology for increasing the probability that you may actually master Life

Balance. *Balance* suggests a steadiness that results when all parts of your life are properly adjusted to each other and when no one part or constituting force outweighs or is out of proportion to another. This system is designed to monitor those proportions and give valuable feedback almost effortlessly.

The Balance Master's Factorial is not a definitive road map, however. At best it is a general set of directions—a set of guidelines, if you will—that can assist you in designing a disciplined system which can best provide you with balance and, additionally or alternatively, give you immediate and useful information when you go out of balance in any area. That information permits you to make changes to get your life moving back into line with your efforts to create Life Balance.

At the back of this book you will find two two-sided cards.[1] Each card is designed for use during a single week. These cards are designed to be both a tactical tool *and* a strategic tool at one and the same time.

LIFE BALANCE FOCUS ITEMS

On the first side of the card is a place for you to list your three most important goals for the upcoming week (see figure 8.1). This is the tactical side of the card in that it allows you to write down a clear statement of your short-term (one-week) intentions. The card also provides you with a place to keep track of a focal partner's three goals for the week, should you choose to work with a focal partner.

You can choose any three weekly goals for yourself from any of your Life Balance categories. It does not matter what you choose so

```
┌──────────────────────────────────────────────────┐
│                                                    │
│   YOUR  FOCUS  ITEMS:                              │
│                                                    │
│   ──────────────────────────────────────────────  │
│                                                    │
│   ──────────────────────────────────────────────  │
│                                                    │
│   ──────────────────────────────────────────────  │
│                                                    │
│   YOUR  PARTNER'S  FOCUS  ITEMS:                   │
│                                                    │
│   ──────────────────────────────────────────────  │
│                                                    │
│   ──────────────────────────────────────────────  │
│                                                    │
│   ──────────────────────────────────────────────  │
│                                                    │
└──────────────────────────────────────────────────┘
```

Figure 8.1. The Balance Master's Factorial Focus Items

long as the goals are important to you. For example, during weeks when I am on vacation, one of the goals is often for me to just relax and enjoy my vacation. When I'm at work, I keep this side of the card faceup on my desk where I can see it every day as a reminder of what I have determined are the three most important things I want to accomplish during the current week.

You may find that working with a focal partner helps you accomplish your goals because that person will keep you accountable. I have been working with the same focal partner now for nearly four years, and the experience has been nothing short of spectacular. Kim and I meet—almost always by telephone—at 7:30 A.M. on Wednesdays, which for a variety of reasons works best for both of us, so our "week" runs from Wednesday morning to Tuesday night. In about thirty minutes, we exchange information on our successes—or lack thereof—with the previous week's three focal items, and we inform each other of the three things we intend to accomplish in the upcoming week. If either of us is out of town or otherwise unavailable at our regular meeting time, we use e-mail instead, which allows for asynchronous communication. Although we live about an hour apart, once in a while we get together for a face-to-face meeting. Those meetings always add a nice personal dimension. I am convinced that my successes these past few years result in large part from sharing my weekly goals with Kim and, at the same time, knowing I will be held accountable for completing them. The last thing we do in our meeting each week is confirm how we will connect the following week.

You may be wondering how to go about finding a focal partner. It isn't hard, really—you begin by just asking people if they are interested in setting up a support system for a period of time, say, three months or so. Decide on the logistics and the ground rules that you will each abide by. Set up your meetings in advance—I've found that it's generally best to keep the connection at the same time every week with an alternative in case one or the other of you is not available, just as Kim and I have done with the e-mail alternative.

You want to find someone who holds a lot of the same values you do in terms of moving his or her life forward and not just talking about it or complaining about it. And you want someone who is willing to be held accountable and willing to hold you accountable. One last thing: Don't be discouraged if you don't find the ideal partner first time out. I went through about a year of trying out different partners, some of whom were good to work with and some of whom could have been better, before Kim and I discovered that we had just the right mix of accountability, discipline, and compassion for each other.

LIFE BALANCE ACTIVITIES

The other side of the cards at the back of the book is called the Balance Master's Factorial Scorecard, and it also has a tactical element to it, but its real value lies in its use as a strategic tool (see figure 8.2).

The Life Balance factorial activities are Meditate, Act, Socialize, Train, Ethos, Reflect, and Sabbath. The initial letters give us a MASTERS factorial, and for Life Balance these Master's Factorials must be repeated weekly, from meditation seven days per week to Sabbath one day per week.

7	MEDITATE						
7	6	ACT					
7	6	5	SOCIALIZE				
7	6	5	4	TRAIN			
7	6	5	4	3	ETHOS		
7	6	5	4	3	2	REFLECT	
7	6	5	4	3	2	1	SABBATH

Figure 8.2. The Balance Master's Factorial Scorecard

The scorecards are designed to allow you to easily keep track of the number of times during the week that you engage in an activity within each factorial as measured against the ideal number of weekly repetitions for that factorial. (If you think about it, this represents to some degree the probability of success in mastering life balance.) At the end of each day, simply mark a box within each factorial for which you had activity that day. While it doesn't matter how you do this, I generally start at the bottom and work up in each column. Regardless of the number of different activities you may have engaged in within a particular factorial, you take credit for any factorial only *once* on any given day. It's something like a punch card in that once you go to a factorial station, your card is punched, and you don't get it punched again by going back to that station on the same day.

You can mark the card in any manner you choose. I find that using a yellow highlighting pen works best for me—I simply color in the box. This is the tactical element of this tool, and it allows you the ability to quickly determine what activities you might want to consider on a particular day to keep your factorial count in balance for the week. Once a column is full, it is full, and additional activities in that factorial for that week are not recorded. For example, a six-month training program for an athletic event I recently completed included training on each of six days during the week, but only the first four were recorded.

At the end of a week, you will find that you have a graphic representation of your activities and the extent to which they contributed or detracted from your personal sense of balance, as in the example of figure 8.3.

7	MEDITATE					
7	6	ACT				
7	6	5	SOCIALIZE			
7	6	5	4	TRAIN		
7	6	5	4	3	ETHOS	
7	6	5	4	3	2	REFLECT
7	6	5	4	3	2	1 SABBATH

Figure 8.3. Example of a completed scorecard

The completed scorecard in figure 8.3 shows a week in which the guidelines for meditation, training, and reflection were met, keeping a Sabbath was ignored, and the other factorials were each a bit short of the ideal.

It's important to note at this stage that no one scorecard will tell you the whole story. A single scorecard is like a single point on a blackboard—it indicates no direction in particular. For example, a scorecard when you are on vacation will look very different from one when you are engaged in a massive work project for which you are putting in many hours on the job, when you are dealing with an important family situation, or while involved in the final stages of a huge charitable event. Each week is likely to be somewhat different from any other simply because of the natural ebb and flow of life's activities, but you can recognize trends by looking at your scorecards for several weeks at once, which is the strategic advantage of the cards.

In my earlier book, *Your Authentic Self: Be Yourself at Work*, I said that I am a strong believer in what I call "management by graphics." This is because the human mind can best capture and assimilate concepts contained in images. This idea is the foundation of the saying "A picture is worth a thousand words." When you look at several scorecards at one time you will see a graphical representation of the level of your Life Balance mastery over time. Exactly where you need to apply intention and attention will also be readily apparent. The only thing remaining, then, is to determine what you will do about any balance issue or other situation you do see.

Let me show you how easy it is to determine where you need to make corrections in your own strategic Life Balance plan. Figure 8.4 shows my completed Life Balance Scorecards for a recent twelve-week period. What do you see?

What you might notice from this array of scorecards is that during this twelve-week period, I had strong commitments to my meditation practice (Meditate × 7), to my work and other goal-oriented activities (Act × 6), and to keeping healthy (Train × 4). During this period I also spent time engaging with family and friends (Socialize × 5), and I did reasonably well participating in activities that contributed to the well-being of my community and to the individuals in it (Ethos × 3).

There are, however, two areas that clearly stand out as needing attention. The first is breaking away from "busy-ness" to look at my life's path and where it's going (Reflect × 2). The other is taking time for rest and communion with Spirit (Sabbath × 1). Notice that there is no need to analyze it or even to think about it—it's readily apparent from the graphical representation of the layout. It hits you immediately.

When I reviewed these cards as part of my own life-balancing process, this realization gave me the opportunity to choose to make some changes, and more importantly, it acted as a catalyst for developing strategies to ensure that those changes actually took place. For example, as a result of reviewing this particular set of scorecards, I started a program of keeping a "reflection journal" in which I make entries at least twice each week. The discipline of keeping the journal forces me to take the time to reflect, and I have not failed to obtain a perfect Reflect × 2 score since I began keeping the journal. As a consequence, my life is somewhat more in balance than it was during the twelve-week period that these cards represent—and it has continued that way. Additionally, I am experiencing the many benefits that a regular program of reflection and planning provides. I have also implemented other strategies to deal with the Sabbath issue, although consistent success there has been harder to obtain.

Each of the individual Balance Master's Factorials is discussed separately in the remaining chapters of this book. While you read and learn about them, remember that these are suggestions only. You might come up with your own set that differs from mine, although my guess is that there would be some significant overlap. Or, even if you determine that your set of factorials is identical to mine, you might include different activities in any given factorial than I do.

The point here is to understand and apply the *process* represented by the Balance Master's Factorial and not necessarily the specifics of it.

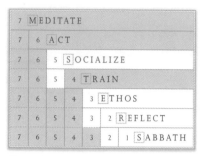

Week 1

7	MEDITATE					
7	6 ACT					
7	6	5 SOCIALIZE				
7	6	5	4 TRAIN			
7	6	5	4	3 ETHOS		
7	6	5	4	3	2 REFLECT	
7	6	5	4	3	2	1 SABBATH

Week 2

7	MEDITATE					
7	6 ACT					
7	6	5 SOCIALIZE				
7	6	5	4 TRAIN			
7	6	5	4	3 ETHOS		
7	6	5	4	3	2 REFLECT	
7	6	5	4	3	2	1 SABBATH

Week 3

7	MEDITATE					
7	6 ACT					
7	6	5 SOCIALIZE				
7	6	5	4 TRAIN			
7	6	5	4	3 ETHOS		
7	6	5	4	3	2 REFLECT	
7	6	5	4	3	2	1 SABBATH

Week 4

7	MEDITATE					
7	6 ACT					
7	6	5 SOCIALIZE				
7	6	5	4 TRAIN			
7	6	5	4	3 ETHOS		
7	6	5	4	3	2 REFLECT	
7	6	5	4	3	2	1 SABBATH

Week 5

7	MEDITATE					
7	6 ACT					
7	6	5 SOCIALIZE				
7	6	5	4 TRAIN			
7	6	5	4	3 ETHOS		
7	6	5	4	3	2 REFLECT	
7	6	5	4	3	2	1 SABBATH

Week 6

7	MEDITATE					
7	6 ACT					
7	6	5 SOCIALIZE				
7	6	5	4 TRAIN			
7	6	5	4	3 ETHOS		
7	6	5	4	3	2 REFLECT	
7	6	5	4	3	2	1 SABBATH

Figure 8.4. Scorecards for a twelve-week period

Week 7

7	MEDITATE					
7	6	ACT				
7	6	5	SOCIALIZE			
7	6	5	4	TRAIN		
7	6	5	4	3	ETHOS	
7	6	5	4	3	2	REFLECT
7	6	5	4	3	2	1 SABBATH

WEEK 7

Week 8

7	MEDITATE					
7	6	ACT				
7	6	5	SOCIALIZE			
7	6	5	4	TRAIN		
7	6	5	4	3	ETHOS	
7	6	5	4	3	2	REFLECT
7	6	5	4	3	2	1 SABBATH

WEEK 8

Week 9

7	MEDITATE					
7	6	ACT				
7	6	5	SOCIALIZE			
7	6	5	4	TRAIN		
7	6	5	4	3	ETHOS	
7	6	5	4	3	2	REFLECT
7	6	5	4	3	2	1 SABBATH

WEEK 9

Week 10

7	MEDITATE					
7	6	ACT				
7	6	5	SOCIALIZE			
7	6	5	4	TRAIN		
7	6	5	4	3	ETHOS	
7	6	5	4	3	2	REFLECT
7	6	5	4	3	2	1 SABBATH

WEEK 10

Week 11

7	MEDITATE					
7	6	ACT				
7	6	5	SOCIALIZE			
7	6	5	4	TRAIN		
7	6	5	4	3	ETHOS	
7	6	5	4	3	2	REFLECT
7	6	5	4	3	2	1 SABBATH

WEEK 11

Week 12

7	MEDITATE					
7	6	ACT				
7	6	5	SOCIALIZE			
7	6	5	4	TRAIN		
7	6	5	4	3	ETHOS	
7	6	5	4	3	2	REFLECT
7	6	5	4	3	2	1 SABBATH

WEEK 12

You should give yourself maximum latitude and flexibility to adjust the system to meet your own personal needs.

You may have realized that the real purpose of the Balance Master's Factorial Scorecards is to help you create new habits in each of the factorial areas. As with the creation of all new habits, at first the activities and even the metrics employed to measure them may seem forced and unnatural. Stick with it! At some point, you will discover that it takes less and less attention for you to do the same things that originally may have been difficult for you to remember or, even when you did remember, to fit into your routine. It will come! Habits, remember, will ultimately keep us on track.

9

Meditate × 7

med•i•tate \'medə,tāt\ *vi* : to keep the mind in a state of
contemplation : dwell in thought : engage in studious reflection;
esp : to practice religious contemplation

TRADITION SAYS THAT MEDITATION was born when Siddhartha Gautama sat beneath a tree about 2,500 years ago and refused to do anything whatsoever until he understood the nature of his own mind and solved the riddle of suffering and pain. After the "Sacred Night," which is said to have lasted some seven weeks, Siddhartha experienced enlightenment and became the Buddha.

Meditation is now widely accepted everywhere—both in Eastern cultures where it has its roots and in Western cultures where it has been accepted, if not always as a religious practice, then at least as a therapeutic and relaxation technique to quiet the mind.

Indeed, the health benefits of meditation continue to be documented by the traditional Western medical establishment. In a study in the *British Medical Journal* in December 2001, physician Luciano

Bernardi, associate professor of internal medicine at the University of Pavia, Italy, reported the results of a study in which the regular recitation of either a prayer (the Ave Maria in Latin) or a mantra ("Om mani padme om," which loosely translates from the Sanskrit, "Harmony is the center of our being") caused striking, powerful, and synchronous increases in existing cardiovascular rhythms.[1]

In short, meditation is *good* for you. It's good for your body, your mind, your emotions, and your spirit. Paramahansa Yogananda, the world-famous author of *Autobiography of a Yogi*, had this to say about meditation in the foreword to his small handbook *Metaphysical Meditations*:

> Meditation is the science of God-realization. It is the most practical science in the world. Most people would want to meditate if they understood its value and experienced its beneficial effects. . . .
>
> Meditation utilizes concentration in its highest form. Concentration consists in freeing the attention from distractions and in focusing it on any thought in which one may be interested. Meditation is that special form of concentration in which the attention has been liberated from restlessness and is focused on God. Meditation, therefore, is concentration used to know God.[2]

Yogananda is absolutely correct. I learned that for myself over thirty years ago when I began a regular practice of meditation. For me, meditation is the one non-negotiable foundation of Life Balance Mastery. You will already have noted that it is the only discipline of the Balance Master's Factorial that is to be practiced each and every day.

Indeed, on those very rare occasions when something happens that prevents me from completing my regular meditation practice first thing in the morning, my day simply does not go right. My energy can be scattered and my responses to events and people can all too frequently be knee-jerk reactions that require a significant amount of cleanup and communication after the fact.

I don't know exactly what it is about meditation that makes it so invaluable to the establishment of Life Balance, but I am very clear on what effect it has on me. Sometimes, when people learn of my habit of sitting in a dark and quiet room for at least thirty minutes immediately upon awakening each morning, their response is something like, "I could never do that!" as though there is some forced effort, mental gymnastics, or even pain involved in practicing meditation. Nothing could be more inaccurate. Meditation does not require any effort; indeed, the practice of meditation is exactly the opposite: it is the complete *absence* of effort.

I frequently hear people mischaracterize meditation as the attempt to empty the mind of *all* thought—and that certainly would be an effort because it is probably not possible, particularly in this day and age. Instead, consider that a discipline of meditation is one in which you simply allow your thoughts to drift into and out of your mind for some specific period of time while you cultivate the habit of letting go. For that meditative period—whether ten, twenty, thirty minutes or longer— you use time-honored techniques for staying present in the moment and allowing your thoughts to enter you or leave you as though they were birds flying in and out of an open castle tower. You force none to stay and none to leave.

There are dozens of techniques for developing a meditation practice. One of the most common is to focus on one's breathing, perhaps counting the breaths and staying mindful of each inhalation and exhalation. Another is to use a mantra, which can be a word that has a specific, repetitive sound like a chant but which may or may not have any meaning. Other alternatives include developing heightened awareness for the immediate surrounding environment in which you find yourself—whether indoors or out. You do this by listening to sounds, noticing smells, and feeling textures. You can also develop a meditative practice by concentrating on the sensory experience of performing common tasks such as washing dishes, sewing, painting, or gardening. At the other extreme, maximum sensory deprivation such as one can experience by floating in a quiet pool of water or lying still in a darkened and quiet room are meditative disciplines practiced by some people. The point is that meditation techniques are many and varied and that there is at least one which will be suitable to your likes and temperament. You simply have to look for it to find it.[3]

The key element of all meditative practices is the development of mindful observation coupled with an absence of control that leads to an ease of existence without needing to be in command and control of everything, as is our normal practice. From meditation we learn to recognize the arbitrary nature of our own thoughts, we see that our judgments about whether those thoughts are "good" or "bad" are themselves arbitrary, we learn to release first the judgments, and then, ultimately, we learn to release the thoughts altogether. We begin to understand that life is a nearly infinite series of such arbitrary thoughts, judgments, and releases. We begin to understand in a visceral way that the pain we suffer in life is directly proportional to the attachment we have to a certain thought or judgment and inversely proportional to our willingness to release that same thought or judgment. In a way, meditation takes us out of habitual reaction and places us in the world of choice.

Michael Chender, a Buddhist teacher and chair of the Shambala Institute, explains it this way:

> Try sitting still for ten minutes and being aware of what's going on around you without getting caught up in particular thoughts about it. Such a seemingly simple thing is difficult to do. You may notice an incessant internal conversation; moment-to-moment you are planning, consoling yourself, chastising yourself, or just chattering aimlessly. We constantly explain the unfolding of experience to ourselves, making sure that everything fits in terms we are comfortable with—deciding with lightning speed what we should accept as supportive, what we should reject as threatening, and what we can safely ignore. This sub-conscious "gossip" colors virtually all of our perceptions and actions, but we are seldom quiet enough to see it. This is the mind we always carry with us, but seldom have the quiet to experience directly.[4]

A direct experience of seeing how your mind works will be a significant advantage to you in every area of your life. Many of us have had the experience of our minds "running away with us," allowing or causing us to say and do things that later, on reflection, we wish we had not said or done. The truth for most people is that their minds *dictate* in the strongest sense of the word their actions and reactions more than they will ever know. Meditation gives you the opportunity to observe how your mind works in terms of its perceptions, prejudices, thoughts, and judgments. From there, you have the ability to choose whether to or how much you wish to rely on that information and how much you want to include data and information from other sources of your intelligence such as your heart, intuition, and spirit.

Make no mistake about it: Your mind will be present in your meditation practice—there is no way to leave it at the entry door, so to speak—and you will find its attempts to gain mastery over the situation and over you to be in attendance there as well. The difference is that one of the stated purposes of your time spent in meditation is to *observe*, and that also means observing your mind and how it operates. You will actually have the opportunity to see through many of its wiles if you are willing to do so.

The trick, of course, is to remain aware—*mindful* is the term most often used in meditation-practitioner circles—during your meditation practice so that when your mind begins to think about the past or future, abstractions, fears, expectations, or worries—the environment in which your mind is most at home—you will be able to recognize what has happened. You can then ever so gently redirect yourself to the mindful activity at hand, namely, observing how your mind works rather than processing real-time the flow of images, thoughts, ideas, and judgments it presents to you for your consumption, reaction, and response.

While it is the observation of how our minds work that is at one and the same time the true essence and value of meditation, that value is not relegated solely to those periods during which you are practicing meditation. The real value lies in the fact that there is significant spill-over of this "observation effect" into your periods of non-meditation. In the midst of some situation—frequently a highly charged one—you will suddenly and surprisingly find yourself in observation of your thought process around that situation. You will gain valuable insights on the situation right then and there, and those insights will help you to safely traverse what would otherwise have been a minefield of con-flicting interests and relationships.

For this to happen, however, it is important to ensure that you develop a true "discipline" of meditation. By "discipline" in this con text I mean *an orderly or regular pattern of behavior*. Meditation must be habitual and consistent for it to be of any benefit to you. The best thing about meditation is that it takes no special tools or props and it can be practiced anywhere you are and at any time.

Mastery of Life Balance is not a phenomenon that is created out-side of you by balancing all your activities in a manner that suits your life direction. More than that, your innermost Being must be in balance with your outermost expression of that Being, and a strong commit-ment to a meditative practice is the only path I know to accomplish that. In the Life Balance Master that commitment is demonstrated by the development of a habit of meditation which includes its practice each and every day.

A commitment to meditation will directly contribute to your Life Balance categories of Health and Fitness and Personal and/or Spiritual

Growth. You will also find that it will strongly, but indirectly, contribute to all the others.

Each week: Meditate times seven. A Balance Master recognizes the importance of communing daily with God, Spirit, Higher Consciousness, the Higher Self—that place of centered peace which is within each one of us.

How will you **Meditate**?

10

Act × 6

act \ˈakt\ *vi* : to carry into effect a determination of the will : take action : MOVE

A LINE FROM FRED SMALL'S uplifting song "Everything Possible" goes, "You can dream all the day never reaching the end of everything possible for you."[1] Each of us creates and defines our own dreams. Perhaps your dreams are about prosperity or your career or your health. Your dream could be closing that key contract at work or getting a long-awaited promotion or new assignment. Your dream could be buying that car you've had your eye on—yes, that one! Dreams can encompass material possessions, relationships with other people and other living beings such as animals, or they can involve revitalized relationships with yourself or Spirit. In the realm of dreams, everything is, indeed, possible, but "possible" doesn't mean "sure thing."

Dreams are wonderful, but dreaming alone isn't enough. To experience success by almost any metric and to achieve the feeling of accomplishment that motivates so many of us, it is imperative that we turn our dreams into realities to whatever extent we are able to do so. Balance Masters recognize that there is a time to dream and a time to take action. They arrange their affairs and their daily lives so that taking action on their dreams is a high priority.

Taking action is what the Act × 6 factorial is all about. It encompasses the various aspects of "doingness" that are involved in so much of life. More than that, however, it is action taken with intention, direction, and discipline. It is the process of planning and then managing with strict attention a course of action that has been calculated by you to get you from where you are to where you want to be. While our dreams are the navigational systems on life's path, our actions in response to and in support of those dreams are the engines that move us forward.

There are many ways to "act" or take action on your dreams. The activity does not need to take all day, but it certainly can. And a day for which you get credit for Act × 6 factorial activities does not have to be entirely or even substantially devoted to such activities. To include a day as one on which you have completed an Act × 6 factorial activity, it is enough if you take some action during the day on one of your goals. As noted above, the action you take does need to be focused and intended to move you closer to your goal. If you are in the habit of making a list of steps to complete a project, it is likely that any of those steps would qualify.

For example, for several years it has been my dream to hold a men's spiritual retreat at a special location here in Northern California. On an unseasonably warm and sunny day a few weeks ago, a friend and I spent the day traveling to one of those sites, reviewed the facility, and met with the conference-center staff. That counted. A few days ago, I ran the financial numbers and determined I could do this and that it would be a reasonably good business proposition. That counted. This morning, I called my staff contact at the conference center, made the reservation, and gave them a deposit. That also counted.

Every time I sat down to write or edit a chapter in this book, it counted as an Act × 6 activity. When I make calls to clients or prepare for a keynote address or a training class, those activities count. On the non-business side, when I make plans for our family dream vacation this year, it counts. Making purchases for a room-redecorating project counts. You determine your dreams. You determine the steps necessary to turn those dreams into reality. And therefore, you determine what qualifies as an Act × 6 activity.

Notice, too, that Act × 6 activities need not be "pure." When my friend John and I traveled up the coast to visit that conference facility, the activity counted not only as an Act × 6 activity but also as a Socialize × 5 activity.

The good news is that this is the easiest of all the factorials to keep up with. We tend to migrate here naturally. Rarely does a week go by in my own life that I do not get a perfect score of six out of six on my scorecard for Act × 6. Unfortunately, the accompanying bad news is that too many of us end up here far too frequently at the expense of the other important elements of our lives. To some extent, the Act × 6 factorial is intended to *limit* our participation in this arena and to remind us to *focus* for maximum results; it is not an exercise to ensure that we do enough of it. Actively working toward your goals six days per week—whatever those goals, whether business or personal—is plenty.

The two essential keys to success in the Act × 6 factorial are planning and focus. When exercised together, these two elements create a balance and harmony within the arena of our actions that make those actions far more productive than if either were practiced alone.

Planning is essential because what you are after here are directed activities that are most likely to give you the results you want. If your dreams are to become realities through your actions, you must learn to plan your work and then you must work your plan through your actions. Planning can be simple or complex, and the need for complexity will vary with the particular goal you have in mind. If you are in Florida and your goal is to get to New York, planning to get in the car to drive north may be sufficient. But if it is your goal while traveling to see the countryside, meet lots of people, and avoid freeways, then you will need to develop a plan with a more refined degree of granularity, and one consisting of heading north on U.S. Route 95 will probably not be enough to get the job done.

Focus is essential because it is the only way to stay on the path of the plan you have developed to turn your dream into reality. Many of us have experienced the frustrations of days in which our activities have been buffeted about by seemingly unending changes in circumstances or priorities. At the end of such days we feel spent, unfulfilled, and adrift while no closer to having achieved our goals. Determined attention to focus can prevent—or at least minimize—those kinds of days.

Think about those times when you have been 100 percent focused. You probably were surprised by how much you were able to accomplish in a short period of time. The secret to those successful, focused days is that you knew exactly what tasks you needed to do and then you did them. More importantly—no, *most* importantly—you didn't allow anything to get in your way and keep you from accomplishing what needed to be done.

In my trainings, workshops, and seminars, I often ask managers and executives to consider what their results would look like if they worked every day—or even part of every day—like they do on the day *before* vacation. We've all had that experience. You know, you have piles and piles of work on your desk—much of which may have been there for weeks waiting for your attention—and you are leaving for a well-deserved vacation the very next morning. Initially, when you sit down to face this monumental task on that last day before vacation, completing it seems impossible, but then something happens, and you start making tremendous strides in getting through the work which needs to be done.

The "something" that happens is *focus*: you *are* going on vacation and nothing—certainly not that pile of work which must be dealt with—is going to stop you! And when you are focused, you suddenly find yourself doing things that at other times you are reluctant or unwilling to do: you prioritize, you delegate, you accept less than absolute perfection from yourself and from others, you are less tolerant of interruptions and time-wasting social visits, you decide there are things you need not do after all, and you allow yourself to say "No!" In the end, you find yourself having been uncommonly—sometimes astonishingly—productive. Focus can be an amazing catalyst on behavior.

There is no reason whatsoever that these usually rare and intermittent moments of focus and productivity cannot become more frequent or, indeed, even your normal manner of operating. What it will take is for you to create—artificially, if necessary—an environment that closely approximates that of the "day before vacation."

You can use the Act × 6 factorial as an excellent tool for creating that environment for yourself. Begin each of your Act × 6 days with a clear vision of what you will be doing that day—and *only* that day—to move one or more of your dreams along their individual paths to realization. Resist the temptation to think you must work on every one of your dreams every day. Write down those actions you will take *today*, keep the list where you can see it, and be relentless in pursuing that course for the day—prevent interruptions, sidestep disruptions, seclude yourself for some period of time if necessary, and otherwise do whatever it takes to remain focused on completing the goals on your list. You need only do this for part of the day to experience a tremendous increase in productivity.

Use the same set of tools that magically appear during your own high productivity "day before vacation" work sessions: prioritize, delegate, be less of a perfectionist, be less tolerant of time-wasting events such as social visits, distinguish between those things that appear urgent but are unimportant and those that truly need emergency attention, consider carefully before choosing to do certain tasks and actually choose not to do some, and learn to effectively say "No!" Interestingly, the ability to demonstrate these skills is what distinguishes superior managers from their mediocre colleagues.

You might want to develop the habit of doing your Act × 6 activities first, in the manner of Stephen R. Covey's Habit Three, "Put First Things First." This is a good habit to establish and will do much to move you along the path from living with your dreams to actually living your dreams.

At the end of a day on which you have participated in any Act × 6 activities, check your progress against your stated goals, see where you might have gone astray or where you could have done better, and carry over to the next day on which you will pursue Act × 6 items those things that you didn't accomplish but are still committed to completing.

Just as Lao-tzu reminds us that a journey of a thousand miles must begin with a single step, you will discover that your journey from the dreams in your heart to the realization and manifestation of those dreams in your life is a series of individual, small, and easy-to-perform steps. Do not focus on finishing the journey, and do not dwell on the distance yet to be traveled. Focus each day instead on beginning—taking the single step that you want to accomplish that day. Once you begin, the energy of starting on your path toward your dreams will carry you through to completion both on that day and in the days ahead.

It's also important to remember that on the one day per week that you do not act, *you do not act!* Not taking action on your dreams on your non-Act × 6 day is as important to your success as is focused action on your Act × 6 days. You will note that the complement to Act × 6 is Sabbath × 1. This is no accident, as you will discover when we discuss Sabbath × 1 later in this book.

You will find that the Act × 6 factorial will contribute to all of your Life Balance categories. For many of us, though, it is most often associated with the categories of Health and Fitness, Money and Finances, Projects and Hobbies, and Work and Career.

Each week: Act times six. After connection through meditation, a Balance Master's next priority is to bring into reality his or her dreams and visions for life in every area: work, play, relationships, possessions, and so on.

On what dreams will you Act?

11

Socialize × 5

> **so·cial·ize** \\'sōshə,līz\ *vi* : to participate actively in a social
> group : enter into or maintain personal relationships with others

WHEN I LOOK AT MY OWN LIFE, I am always amazed by how few
of the many activities I engage in with family and friends truly qualify
as genuine socialization. I think this is true for most people. Sur-
rounded by family and friends as we are much of the time, we think
that there are no limits to our opportunities for socialization, and this
is certainly true. But the fact that opportunities are limitless does not
mean that we avail ourselves of those opportunities. Indeed, most of us
have made an unconscious discipline of ignoring or at least not taking
full advantage of those opportunities as we go about occupied with
life's "busyness."

It is well established that humans are social beings. Research is
legion on the effects of the deprivation of social interaction on
infants, children, and adults, and it has been clearly indicated that an

active social network is essential to our well-being. We do not do especially well as isolated islands, and our ability to live fully and thrive emotionally is a function of the social-support networks we create for ourselves.

The situation is further complicated and exacerbated by the pace at which most of us live these days. Many homes feel more like airline or bus terminals with people coming and going at all hours of the day and night and few times, if any, when everyone is present so that meaningful and heartfelt conversations and social intercourse can take place, all of which are essential to creating a sense of familial community.

Interestingly, despite the proximity of family and friends, the Socialize × 5 factorial may be the most difficult of all to master. This is true for several reasons. First, it takes a real effort to make it happen. It almost always takes some planning, and in today's hectic world, it may require *significant* planning. That's not to say that there can't be or won't be spontaneous Socialize × 5 activities, but relying on spontaneity entirely is not likely to give you the five experiences of socializing you will want each week. Remember, the goal here is to develop this factorial into a habit.

Second, your attempts to meet the Socialize × 5 factorial requirements can be somewhat insidious in that too many things masquerade as socializing but really aren't socializing at all. Dragging the kids to the supermarket, watching television with the family in which there is little interaction other than someone asking that the volume be turned up or down, taking silent car trips in which everyone is into his or her own thing, and doing separate chores around the house albeit at the same time are only a few of the types of activities that come to mind as counterfeit socializing events. Another related issue is that far too many people confuse the Act × 6 factorial with this one. They operate under the mistaken belief that doing things *for* the important people in their lives—which frequently involves earning money and obtaining life's necessities and niceties—is the same thing as doing things *with* the important people in their lives. This phenomenon goes a long way to explain how so many people—men in particular—are surprised to find late in a life spent in pursuit of material possessions for their families that they are irreconcilably estranged from the very people for whom they put in those many years of effort. In these situations the mirrored feelings of betrayal on the parts of the breadwinner and his estranged spouse and/or children are as understandable as they are tragic. These men feel unappreciated because they spent their lives pursuing a sense of security and a good life for their families; in the meantime, their families, while experiencing and sometimes even expressing gratitude for that sense of security and the lifestyle it engenders, feel cheated because in their view the most important thing the man had to give was withheld from them: himself. As women have begun to fill the roles traditionally reserved to men, they are also beginning to experience some of the same effects, although it is still somewhat early in the game to draw any real conclusions. Perhaps and hopefully, they will do better.

The third reason that mastering the Socialize × 5 factorial is so difficult is that, unlike any of the other factorials, you cannot do this one alone, and that single difference complicates matters significantly. As noted above, the initial and perhaps simplest level of complication is that of calendaring Socialize × 5 activities at times when you and those with whom you want to socialize—particularly family members—are available. Further complications can arise around the *nature* of those activities. I remember my father's attempts to spend "Dad time" with my brother and me being thwarted—from my perspective at least—by the fact that my dad's idea of spending time with his boys was to throw a baseball around, and that was something I just didn't care to do at all. I did it, but I was never fully engaged. As a consequence, instead of those episodes of ball playing strengthening our relationship as I know my father intended them to do, they fed a slowly smoldering resentment in me that I was too young to recognize or do anything about.

The important thing to understand is that it is not the nature of the pursuits which matters so long as the activity chosen is one that each member of your family or circle of friends enjoys. Pursuits can be active or they can be more sedentary. Like many families, my wife and daughter and I have had deep connections doing things together as diverse as hiking, cycling, and swimming in the ocean on the one hand and playing a board game, working on arts and crafts, or quietly reading together on the other. The crucial element these activities must have is the one key word both of the phrases in the previous sentence have in common: *together*.

First and foremost, the Socialize × 5 factorial requires a high degree of togetherness—conscious, vigorous, and mindful togetherness. This contributes to what the underlying foundation of this factorial is: getting to know each other better and more deeply, learning from each other, supporting one another, sharing good and difficult times, and witnessing each other's growth. The buzzword for this in the 1980s and 1990s was "quality time." I cannot tell you what "quality time" will mean to you and to those in your circle of friends and family, although I know what it means to me and to those around me in my various social groups. Just so, you will know what it means to you, and your family and friends will know what it means to them with respect to their individual relationships with you. Note, though, that you may have to actually ask to find out—more than once and in more than one way.

Recognize, too, that the concept of socializing will not only mean different things to different people, but it will mean different things to the same people over time. For example, the activities of socialization involving my now fifteen-year-old daughter have changed dramatically since she was a toddler, and there have already been several turnovers to new activities from that time to this. I expect, too, that these activities will continue to change as she grows into her later teen years and into young adulthood. At the same time, there are certain things that have remained very much the same, like golden threads that bind us together for all time. And this is what practicing the Socialize × 5 factorial is also about—finding out what those threads are, making a conscious effort to create time and opportunities for them, and watching and responding appropriately as they evolve over time.

Some of these activities have now become timeless rituals that we continue to keep, and the very act of keeping them together contributes to the unique sense of family we feel. For example, when my daughter was very little, we began a tradition that has remained substantially unchanged. On the Friday after Thanksgiving, we begin unpacking the Christmas boxes. The first thing we always take out is the box marked "Advent Wreath," in which there are four jeweled candleholders and a large collection of baubles, glittering strands of beads, artificial fruits and berries, and a sixteen-inch artificial evergreen wreath. Each year, my daughter and I create a unique Advent wreath using the materials in the box. We add only four new candles each year, which are used up during the Advent season. Each evening during Advent the three of us sit around the table on which the wreath is placed, light the appropriate candle or candles, and read aloud from a booklet of Advent readings sent to us annually by a metaphysically-oriented Christian movement. One evening many years ago, when my daughter was just beginning to read, she asked if she could do the reading, and we listened patiently as she struggled with the new and difficult words. She's been doing those readings every night during Advent ever since, and my wife and I have listened as her confidence and her voice have grown stronger each year. Someday, I know, my daughter will bring others to that wreath-adorned table or she will create one of her own—either way, the connection between us all will still be there.

This example underscores the lasting importance of the Socialize × 5 factorial. I am certain that you have similar examples from your own life. The point is that you must create, re-create, and celebrate those moments because each one has the potential to develop into a memory that connects us at a visceral level in a way that nothing else can.

Recognize that the same approach can be used with friends, and interestingly, coordinating the friends side of the equation can often be easier than the family side. For reasons that have never been fully clear to me, many of us find the time to do things with friends that help build deep relationships, but we are unable to do the same thing with family members. That may be a function of simply taking family members for granted or a recognition that relationships with friends need to be managed and nurtured to thrive. Indeed, if many of us simply took the same care in managing our relationships with family members as we do in managing our relationships with friends, the entire Socialize × 5 factorial would probably take care of itself.

Take a moment to consider what activities you do now with family and friends that can serve as the core for a set of Socialize × 5 factorial activities. Whether you are participating in those activities in a mindful way now or not does not matter so long as when you do intentionally include them as part of your Socialize × 5 factorial you do so in a conscious and mindful way—again, with an eye to creating and deepening relationships with your circle of family and friends. Next, come up with a list of Socialize × 5 activities that you are not yet doing but would like to do. Then, give each one a try. You may be surprised to discover that you have the makings of a ritual of some significance to yourself and others, such as the annual Advent ritual is to my family and me.

The complement to the Socialize × 5 factorial is Reflect × 2. While it is certainly important for us to develop our deepest connections with others, it is also important for us to turn away from such interactions on occasion for the purpose of aligning with our own individual paths. There is a need for balance between an external focus (socializing) and an internal focus (reflection), as we will see in chapter 14, "Reflect × 2."

You will find that the Socialize × 5 factorial will make its strongest contributions to your Life Balance categories of Community and Contribution, Family and Friends, Fun and Frolic, and Health and Fitness. You will also discover that applying the principles of the Socialize × 5 factorial in your workplace will contribute to greater success in your Work and Career category.

Each week: Socialize times five. A Balance Master rejoices in entering into and maintaining personal relationships with others— both family and friends. Circles of love create circles of energy that support a Balance Master in all areas of life.

With whom will you **Socialize**?

12

Train × 4

DON'T CONFUSE TRAINING WITH EXERCISE. They have very little in common, except, perhaps, for the fact that a lot of the activity for each involves participation of your physical body as a fundamental element and, as a consequence, oftentimes both lead to physical fitness. But that's where the similarities end.

To me, the concept of "exercise" has always somehow been related to fear of one kind or another—you know, the fear of gaining or regaining weight or of heart disease or diabetes or of simply laying bare the effects of advancing age. In my own experience, the idea of exercise has always had an almost punitive edge to it. In the days that I attempted to "exercise" on a regular basis, thoughts like, "If I don't run, I'm going to get fat!" or "My mother died of heart disease; I'd better do something to prevent that happening to me!" ran through my mind. While it was a choice, it always felt like a choice between the lesser of two evils.

Exercise seemed to be more about looking back over my shoulder—running *from* something. It was baseball great Satchel Paige who remarked, "Don't look back. Something might be gaining on you." A lot of people I know exercise in that spirit. You can hear it in the choice of words they use when they talk about their participation in physical activities: "I *have* to go to the gym" and "I'd *better* go run before it gets any later."

And indeed, to a certain extent, fears like these can act as strong motivators to get us up off the couch and doing something physical, but they are *never* long-term motivators. At some point, we get comfortable with a fear—or we begin to see the outcome we fear as inevitable, so the presence of the fear no longer motivates us to do anything. We might think, "I'm going to get old and frail eventually, so why bother?"

I no longer exercise. I *train*. The difference is that training is a forward-looking, future-oriented proposition. It's not about running away or keeping at bay something you fear; it's about moving toward a goal—even an arbitrary one—that has been set up in advance.

What converts what would otherwise be "exercise" into "training" for me is that the objective of each physical-activity session is oriented toward getting me ready for some future event I have chosen to participate in. Sometimes the event is a solo cross-desert hike of four or five days running; sometimes it is a cross-country ski trip through backcountry with a group of friends; sometimes it's a five- or six-hundred-mile bicycle ride or a marathon to raise money for an AIDS organization or some other charity. It doesn't matter what the event is so long as I am interested in doing it because I find it exciting, it is a "stretch" of some degree in terms of my present physical condition, and most importantly, I have sufficient time to ready myself for the event by a program of regular, disciplined training.

There is another positive by-product of the Train × 4 factorial, and that is the development of self-discipline. The key, of course, is to ensure that the flavor of self-discipline you create for yourself is both gentle and, at the same time, effective.

At this stage of my life, I *always* have an event scheduled—entry fee paid and date reserved on my calendar—somewhere on the horizon, with the result that I am always in training for something. Indeed, as soon as a scheduled event looms close on the calendar, I begin the search for the next. I know that if I don't overlap my motivating events, I'll lose my hard-won training momentum.

Sometimes my training program is one in which I train entirely alone. Sometimes I participate in a group training program whose sole purpose is to get folks ready for a particular event, such as the National AIDS Marathon Training Program (*aidsmarathon.org*). Those organized programs can provide extra motivation and stimulus through the conscious creation of a community with a common goal. Sometimes my training is a combination of both. The specific training arrangement doesn't matter because the shift from an exercise mentality to a training mentality is an internal one. As I said earlier, the activities involved in exercise and training may look identical; it's the mind-set that makes all the difference.

An "in training" mentality begins with selecting a future event for which you will, well, train. Pick some activity that requires you to move beyond your present physical capabilities. If you've never run a mile, then choose something like a 5K or 10K event. If you are fairly active already, choose something you haven't done yet, such as a marathon or half-marathon or a "century" (100-mile) bike ride. What the activity is and how long or strenuous it is need be only a reflection of your interests combined with your present level of expertise and fitness. Remember, you want to stretch your capabilities.

It can be even more fun if the event that you select is something in which you have no real expertise or that you are having a hard time imagining yourself completing. For example, when I signed up to participate in my first AIDS Ride several years ago, which meant riding a bicycle about six hundred miles from San Francisco to Los Angeles, I didn't even own a bicycle and the task looked more than formidable— it looked impossible! There is a lot to be said for working toward breaking through your perceived limitations. That kind of success spills over into other, nonphysical areas of your life such as increasing your self-confidence and developing trust in your own abilities and potential.

There are hundreds if not thousands of possible events in dozens of different athletic pursuits and for just about any level of participant— from the beginner who doesn't know the first thing about the activity to an expert who is seeking to move into the highest levels of competition in the field. There are programs and events for walkers as well as programs and events for accomplished tri-athletes. Just one search on the Internet will provide you with event listings, calendars, entry forms, training programs and schedules starting at all levels of proficiency, and lists of support and training organizations enough to last you a lifetime. All you need do is choose an event, sign up for it, and then commit to and start your training.

Recognize, too—and this is important—that you don't have to enter some formal "authorized" sporting event or competition. You can set things up on your own for yourself or for a group of friends. My treks across the desert are like that. The only things that I arrange well in advance are the starting and ending dates. The other details—where will I start from, where will I end up, how will I get there, how will I get back, and so on—are all determined as part of the training. The key is to have something in your future—formal or informal—to which you are committed and for which it is necessary for you to train.

A word of caution is probably in order here. Many people are driven by an urge to compete—if not with others, then with themselves. For example, I have a friend nearly my age who runs marathons and whose mind-set is that he needs to constantly keep improving his performance. Clearly, over a lifetime, that is an impossibility. Let me tell you from my own experience that at fifty-four years of age, my finishing time in the marathon I will be running in just a few weeks in Honolulu will be *significantly* longer than my finishing time was when I ran in the San Francisco Marathon in 1978 when I was not quite thirty years old.

Instead, select your event from the perspective of where you are "right now"—meaning at the time of selection of the event. What is the level of your ability in that activity? You should view the future event with some mild degree of trepidation about your ability to actually complete it. This will let you know that it's a stretch for you. On the other hand, don't choose the impossible. The gap between where I am now and my ability to climb Mount Everest is much too wide to be bridged in a year's time—maybe even too wide for a two- or three-year training period or at all, and making those kinds of plans makes no sense because they will almost certainly result in failure and, as with any plans on my part to climb Mount Everest, could be dangerous or even deadly.

Basing your choice on your present condition also allows you to take into account several other factors such as all the things going on in the rest of your life. If you are in a period in your life in which other Life Balance categories are likely to require significant attention, for example, if you are expecting a child, if you will be moving your home, or if you expect to be changing jobs, you will want to choose something that requires less training time—meaning something that you feel more ready to do now and that will require less of a stretch.

This approach also allows you to take into account recent events. One year, for example, I was recovering from a fairly serious accident, and the selection of "easy" events during that period reflected my need to continue to heal while still continuing to train. No matter what is going on in your life, you still need to be in training, but you can cut yourself some slack by choosing an activity more in line with your then-present and existing capabilities.

The key point here is to learn not to get caught up in a competitive-based "I-have-to-improve-my-last-performance" mentality. At some point—even if it takes until you are ninety—you simply will not be able to do that, and then what will be your motivation? Training is a concept that should last your lifetime, and you don't want to develop a motivation mind-set that will work against you at the time you will most want it working for you. Remember, training is a state of mind, and creating that mental state is what you are after.

I find that training four times per week is essential—three times feels too much like my old "exercise" days, and for me, that fourth day makes all the difference. What I mean by "training" in this context is "doing something that moves me to my ultimate goal of completing the event I have chosen to do." Not all of any week's training sessions necessarily need to be physical in nature, or if they are all, in fact, physical, they need not be equally demanding. For example, my six-month marathon-training program has included running one very long run each week—usually with the organized training group on Saturday or Sunday—plus two shorter maintenance runs on my own each week and some type of cross-training at least three times per week, which, as the months have gone by, has moved from indoor weight training to outdoor swimming and then to walks in the beautiful autumnal countryside.

Another aspect included automatically in the Train × 4 factorial that is generally missing from "exercise" as we generally know it is nutrition. It is hard to be in training for a future event and also not watch your diet and nutrition—doing so is a natural by-product. The body knows its own needs, and if you are on a regular training program, you will have the opportunity to become aware of your body's nutritional needs. For example, your intake of water—highly recommended in nearly every dietary discipline—will naturally increase. You are likely to find yourself eating fewer snacks and reaching for healthy snacks when you do choose to have one.

Don't wait to commit to some future athletic event until you feel like being more active or until you've actually gotten "good enough" at something, which you think will make you feel more motivated. It actually works the other way around: Committing to an event will motivate you to train, and that training will give you the impetus and energy to be more active. Then the regular practice of your new athletic discipline—whatever it is—will result in you becoming better at it. Don't move to the next chapter in this book until you have selected a future event, signed up for it, and committed to start to train for it. Then, follow through!

The complement to the Train × 4 factorial is Ethos × 3. Training is very much directed inward in that you will be focused on the experience of your body, how it feels, and what it is capable of doing. It is the ultimate in "self-centeredness" in that you are taking care of yourself totally. As we will see in the next chapter, the Ethos × 3 factorial is about taking care of others.

You will find that the activities involved in your commitment to train can contribute to the categories of Community and Contribution, Family and Friends, Health and Fitness, Personal and/or Spiritual Growth, and Projects and Hobbies in your Life Balance equation.

Each week: Train times four. A Balance Master moves beyond fitness or exercise to the forward impetus known as "training." To train is to experience the full power and miracle of the human body's abilities.

For what will you Train?

13

Ethos × 3

> **ethos** \\'ē͜ˌthäs\\ *n* : the disposition, fundamental outlook, moral attitude, or system of values of an individual

WHEN YOU DO CERTAIN THINGS, it just feels good to do them. These things can be planned and organized, or they can occur in an instant when you spontaneously take advantage of some spur-of-the-moment opportunity.

These activities can involve the giving of money or other items of value, or they can be as simple as gifts of your time. They can involve hundreds or even thousands of people, or they can occur between you and just one other person. They can involve people you know and love, or they can concern people you've never met and who live on the other side of the planet.

The word *ethos* comes from the Greek ῆθος, or *ēthos*, meaning "moral character," and its use here is intended in the most expansive manner possible, to include all the elements of the discipline that deals with doing what feels right and the concepts of moral duty that are incorporated in the original meaning of the word.

Whatever the circumstances, all Ethos × 3 activities have one thing in common: They are all based in the heart. I've mentioned elsewhere in this book that our lives are made up as much by the relationships we create as anything that resides totally within us. Indeed, I submit that who we are at heart is, to some major degree, a function of those relationships. This is the core of the Ethos × 3 factorial—looking into your heart and doing what feels right to you to do. It requires significant introspection and intuition, both of which are important tools of Balance Masters.

Ethos × 3 activities emphasize your connection to people, because it is nearly impossible to perform true Ethos × 3 activities from any place other than the heart. Moreover, because Ethos × 3 activities are fueled by generosity, when you act on them, they stimulate abundance and fulfillment in your own life.

Ethos × 3 activities are often about how you take care of other people. These are the kinds of activities that are traditionally thought of as "charitable" or "philanthropic." Supporting charitable organizations and their activities is only one method, but it is a good one and the place most of us start. You can do this in a variety of different ways: You can volunteer your time and talents working directly with the people who need caring assistance; you can donate money; you can raise funds for charitable organizations, put on events, or do office or clerical work or even manual labor.

There is literally no end to the organizational opportunities available to you to work Ethos × 3 activities into your life. Some people use their professional skills relatively unchanged: lawyers do legal work, accountants do financial accounting work, salespeople do fund-raising, and the like. Others take the road of performing tasks that they otherwise would have little or no opportunity to do in their "regular" lives: doctors stuff envelopes, business executives do manual labor, teachers serve meals, and so on. Personally, I have found a mix of both extremes to my liking. In the past I have used my background in law and strategic planning to work as an organization's corporate secretary, to deal with its legal issues, or to serve on its board of directors. At other times, I have hammered nails at the direction of a construction supervisor, made thousands of photocopies, served meals in a soup kitchen, and even cleaned toilets. I've enjoyed all of it just about equally, because it's not the nature of the duties that counts here. It's the circumstances—the underlying ethos—of giving freely of yourself, your time, and your talents that creates a sense of personal satisfaction and self-fulfillment such as nothing else can.

But it should be noted here that when you are considering what you will do in your organizational charity work, *don't just do what's easiest!* For example, if you have plenty of money in your bank account, don't restrict your Ethos × 3 activities to writing checks—write *some* checks, by all means—but for the sake of your own personal growth and sense of fulfillment, seek to include some activities in your Ethos × 3 factorial that require something more than little or no effort on your part. Stretching yourself to perform these activities and experiencing the power they engender in you when you succeed is part of the gift they bring to you and why it is so important for Balance Masters to perform them on a regular basis.

And by all means, don't limit your Ethos × 3 activities to organizational programs. You will be amazed at the amount of relief, support, comfort, and joy you can bring into the life of an elderly or disabled neighbor with an occasional visit. An afternoon spent visiting a senior home facility for simple conversation or reading aloud will repay you in ways you cannot imagine. I know people who use their special talents—storytelling, performing magic, playing cards, organizing group activities—to create memorable and joyful experiences for people who are living in difficult circumstances such as long-term-care hospital wards and hospices.

Be creative. In looking for opportunities to exercise the Ethos × 3 factorial, allow whimsy to take you where it will. Consider leaving a small anonymous gift on the desk of a co-worker—and maintain your anonymity. You can quietly and secretly pay for a stranger's meal in a restaurant, watch his or her surprise and delight when the server explains that the meal has been paid for, and experience for yourself a feeling that cannot be explained in words. Pay the toll for the car behind you. Be as silly as you dare to be—no, be *sillier* than you have ever dared to be! You will be amazed at the depth of your passion and creativity when you get into the spirit and rhythm of looking for ways to add joy—even in the smallest amounts—to other people's lives.

You can only just begin to imagine the positive impact your actions can have on others, and there is a fantastic—almost magical—rippling effect that occurs. You touch people and their lives are made brighter; those people then touch others in a different way than they otherwise would have and they, in turn, make those others' lives brighter. I know you've participated in this chain reaction many times in your life. What you may not have realized before is the extent to which you can *start*

that chain reaction all by yourself. You don't need anyone to do anything nice to or for you first. When you take the initiative, you create
positive energy that fills you and the other person. You both leave the
interaction—including and especially anonymous interactions—with
that positive energy, and then you both share that with others who, in
turn, do the same. It's like lighting your own candle and then sharing
your flame to light the candle of another, who does the same, and so on.
You will never know how many candles your candle has lit, but you
know in your heart that it's many.

If you are smart about this, the things that make up your own set
of Ethos × 3 activities will vary from week to week. You certainly can
have a regular "gig" somewhere, but you really want to avoid falling
into the doldrums of a routine around any of these activities. You know
the exercise, "It's Sunday, so I have to go see Aunt Martha at the con-
valescent home." In truth, the energy of an "obligation" mind-set is
inconsistent with the spirit of Ethos × 3 activities in the manner in
which you will want to experience them. Don't waste these opportunities on what you see as obligations.

Finding three activities based in Ethos each week will help in this
regard. It's too easy to turn a single such activity into a once-a-week
obligation. (Think "Aunt Martha.") Twice a week is better, but it's still
possible to fall into a routine mind-set. However, finding three such
opportunities each week gives you a fighting chance to come up with
something spontaneous. And those spontaneous activities are the true
source of power of the Ethos × 3 factorial.

Going through life in mindful awareness of looking for ways—
right now, this very moment—that you can be of service, do something

nice, be generous, provide a boost to someone's mood, or any one of the other ways you can meet the Ethos × 3 requirement is an astounding place from which to experience life. It has the capacity to change everything about your view of yourself and your life circumstances— even your perception of your past and your future. Unless you already live a very regulated and disciplined life, you will be forced to increase your level of awareness on a daily basis in order to accumulate three Ethos × 3 activities each week, and *that* is a good thing.

You will notice, over time, that you actually receive a great deal more in just about every conceivable way than you give in these circumstances. At about that same time, you will also probably find that this behavior has become an ingrained habit that you will not want to break.

The complement to the Ethos × 3 factorial, in which you are doing things for others, is the Train × 4 factorial, in which you are doing things exclusively for yourself so that you can reach your own personal goals.

You will find that exercising the Ethos × 3 factorial will contribute to your Life Balance categories of Community and Contribution, Family and Friends, and Personal and/or Spiritual Growth.

Each week: Exercise ethos times three. A Balance Master acts on his or her individual sense of moral purpose, guiding beliefs, ethical standards, and ideals to make the world a better place for everyone.

How will you express your individual Ethos?

14

Reflect × 2

> **re•flect** \rə'flekt\ *vt* : to remember with thoughtful consideration
> : come to recollect, realize, or consider in a course of thought :
> think quietly and calmly

MANY OF US SPEND much of our time with our noses to the grindstone in one form or another. We make huge investments of time and
attention to move our personal agendas forward. Admittedly, these
agendas are the very "stuff" of life and often lead to the deepening of
personal relationships and the acquisition of material things that we
envision for our futures. Indeed, the activities that forward our personal agendas are purposefully included in the system of the Balance
Master's Factorial in the form of the Act × 6, Socialize × 5, Train × 4,
and Ethos × 3 factorials.

However, I know from my own experience that failing to reflect
and check in with myself—my Inner Self—on a regular basis while
engaging in the activities that will move my personal agenda forward
can have potentially disastrous results. I've been saved from this fate by

Providence on several occasions—and sometimes I haven't been—and those close calls have reinforced in me the need to stop, disengage from my labors, and take a good look around on a regular basis to see if the path that I am on is still actually the one that I *want* to be on. More than one of these providential events has dramatically changed the course of my life.

For example, for as long as I can remember, there was a consensus in my family that I would become a medical doctor. It's not exactly clear to me where this idea came from—whether it was one I came up with myself or whether it was simply another aspect of outer-centered-reality training to which I acquiesced at a very early age.[1] Nevertheless, I can no longer remember the source. Suffice it to say, however, that throughout high school—and even in junior high school—my nose was firmly applied to the grindstone that would lead me to a career in medicine. I took what were then known as "academic" courses supplemented only by those "electives" that were required to graduate.

My choice of university and the course of study I took there ("premed") were also geared exclusively toward this goal, and I steadfastly applied myself to studying and getting good grades in the sciences to facilitate my acceptance into a top-notch medical school.

Nearly everything in my life at that time was about readying me for the practice of medicine. I spent the summer after my first year in college working in a hospital in my hometown and did the same thing the next summer. The summer before my final year in college, I stayed in Washington, D.C., where I attended school and worked at one of the big city hospitals.

Then, as I said, Providence intervened to give me additional information as well as some much-needed time for reflection. In January of my senior year I worked as a temporary registrar in the university's Office of the Dean of Students. On the second day of registration and much to my chagrin, I found that I was pretty much held captive in an environment in which there was little work to do for a period of nearly ten hours. I wasn't prepared for this turn of events and had not brought anything of my own to do. One of my co-workers, a first-year law student at the university, had been through the exercise before and had had the foresight to bring along personal reading material, which consisted of his law books. Since I had absolutely nothing to do, I borrowed a couple of them and began reading. My excitement over what I read prompted me to seriously question the decision I had made a decade or more before to follow a career in medicine. After a few more months of thinking and investigation, I chose instead a career in law. And that, to borrow from poet Robert Frost, has made all the difference.

We sometimes get so involved in taking action to make something happen that we forget everything else, including asking ourselves such questions as, Is this something I still want to have happen? None of us is immune from this phenomenon—we all do it, albeit to different degrees. Other times, such as when the universe doesn't seem to be supporting us, we take it as a challenge that must be overcome—and at nearly any cost—rather than see it as a possible sign that we should re-examine what we are doing. Sometimes Higher Powers intervene as they did in my choice of career; sometimes they don't, so we can't always count on that happening.

And that is the purpose of the Reflect × 2 factorial. It is intended to be a regular, self-imposed opportunity to remove your nose from that all-important grindstone and look up, outward, and forward into the future as far as you can possibly see, or farther if you have the imagination to do so.

There are many benefits to doing this. First, as pointed out above, it is possible to get so involved in the individual steps of a particular course of action toward a goal that you may not be aware that you or the circumstances around you have changed and that the sought-after goal—appropriate and laudable as it might still be—no longer appeals to you in the way it once did. Maybe the course you are on is just perfect. Maybe it's only OK. Maybe it's not. The point is that you will never know if you don't make a habit of occasionally stopping and taking a look at where you are going and how you feel about it.

The second reason that reflection is important is as simple as knowing where you are going. Even if your goals and dreams do remain the same, it is imperative to look up from the pavement once in a while to make sure you are still on course. Imagine, if you can, how difficult it would be to walk several blocks to a friend's house if you spent the entire time looking down at your feet. Silly as this seems, it is exactly what many of us do while traveling from where we are to where we want to be in our lives: We look exclusively at the individual steps we take without checking in once in a while with the big picture. We go, as it were, from tree to tree without understanding where we may be with respect to the forest.

Third, Reflect × 2 sessions are invitations to dream. You may remember from chapter 10 that I said that dreams are wonderful but that dreaming is not enough, hence the need for the Act × 6 factorial. Dreams *are* wonderful, and they *are* necessary. Living a life overflowing with activity but none of which is responsive to or in furtherance of one's dreams would be a very dreary existence indeed! Some dreams come to us spontaneously, some come to us through the subtle or not-so-subtle suggestions of others, but the dreams that count—those which really motivate us in ways nothing else can—are those dreams that rise up from within ourselves as great yearnings and desires for and visions of our future. There is something wonderfully otherworldly about the nature of those dreams. They speak to us in voices, tones, and harmonies that are unique to us and that often only we can understand.

A fourth and very important reason for undertaking a regular program of reflection is that it gives us the opportunity to delve into the depths of wisdom. To understand this, I need to explain a phenomenon that has begun to plague us only in the last half-century.

For the first dozen millennia or so that humans began gathering into various forms of civilization—tribes, agrarian communities, towns, cities, nations—what people passed from generation to generation was *wisdom*. Wisdom can best be described as the intelligent application of learning. Wisdom was revered for its straightforward simplicity and never-failing reliability. And over time, wisdom remains relatively unchanged in both quality and quantity.

Also passed on were some key elements of *knowledge*. Knowledge applies to any body of known facts or a system of ideas inferred from such known facts. In the earliest days of our history, knowledge tended to be based on natural phenomena such as the timing of the tides, the seasons, the flooding of rivers, and so on. Knowledge became more complex and specialized with each passing age as the development of the sciences, the arts, and commerce and industry progressed.

What was in short supply in the ancient world was *data*, which is detailed information of any kind. In the ancient world, people tended to reflect on and depend on wisdom and to apply knowledge as it was relevant to their lives, but they saw little value in the acquisition of data.

The relationship of wisdom, knowledge, and data in the ancient world was generally pyramidal, as depicted in figure 14.1.

Figure 14.1. The Ancient World

About halfway through the last century—yes, I mean just a little over fifty years ago, although many would argue that the time frame is actually much shorter than that—the ratio between these three elements started to change dramatically. We suddenly found and continue to find ourselves completely overwhelmed with data, which is now more commonly called information. At the same time, bodies of knowledge started to expand geometrically in every direction and have continued to grow with no end in sight. As an example, when I was a child in the 1950s, nearly every doctor in town was a general practitioner. Try to find one in your town today.

While the amount of wisdom has not decreased by any means, the enormous volume of data and knowledge that demands our attention on a daily basis has simply crowded it out. When was the last time you let yourself sit on a hillside watching the stars slowly turning on a clear night or the clouds gently drifting by on a sunny day and pondered the truths and wisdom of the universe?

The relationship of data, knowledge, and wisdom in the modern world looks very much like figure 14.2. Notice that the amount of wisdom has remained relatively constant but that the ratio between the elements has changed drastically.

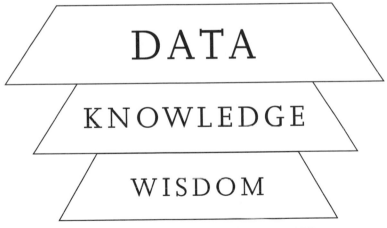

Figure 14.2. The Modern World (post circa 1950)

And this is the real reason why the Reflect × 2 factorial is so important to Balance Masters: If we do not arrange our lives to *force* time for reflection, it simply will not happen because we will be overwhelmed by the onslaught of data and knowledge, and we run the risk of completely losing our connection to wisdom, particularly that wisdom which comes from within us.

How you go about spending your Reflect × 2 time is entirely up to you. You can look at your entire life or just one element of it. Some people like a formal approach in which they review and write out their accomplishments for the week and then write out their goals for the next week. Others prefer a more relaxed, informal approach in which they gently sift through the experiences of the recent past or allow them to come, unforced, into their consciousness. This is not unlike the method used in meditation, except that there is an element of direction to the thoughts and images in reflection that is avoided in a meditation experience.

Some people prefer to have their Reflect × 2 sessions alone; others like group activities or the opportunity to work with a focal partner on a regular basis. Some combine reflection with other Balance Master's factorials. For example, some of my best periods of reflection have occurred while I am participating in a long run or bicycle ride as part of a Train × 4 activity. Another excellent way of managing this process is to start a "reflection journal" into which you enter your thoughts and insights—all you need to do is to make two entries each week and you've completed your Reflect × 2 requirement.

Whichever methodology you use, and even if you go from one to another over time, consider including the following elements:

- Get a sense of where you are on your personal path. Gauge how far you have come and acknowledge yourself for having come that distance already.

- Ask what is new or different about your situation, your feelings, and your intended path.
- Re-establish your connection with the energy of your path. Determine if you or your circumstances have changed and whether the path you started on will still lead you to the dreams that are right for you.
- Consider what things you did that you really feel good about having done for yourself or for others. If there are some things you think you could have done better, consider what you might have done differently.
- With respect to any difficult situation, ask yourself the Four Questions: Why this? Why me? Why now? What am I to learn from this? Listen for any answers that may come, then or later.
- Listen for intuitive wisdom.
- Review your Balance Master's Factorial Scorecard results and determine whether or not you are meeting your own expectations in that regard.

This need not take a lot of time. Sometimes the things that bubble to the surface of your consciousness first are the most important, so consider those carefully without necessarily looking for deeper reasons or meanings. The point is to take the time to perform the ritual of reflection. You will be amazed at what you will find out about yourself and about your journey.

As pointed out in an earlier chapter, the complement factorial to Reflect × 2 is Socialize × 5. The latter emphasizes an external focus, while the emphasis of the former is internal.

You will find that the Reflect $\times$ 2 factorial will actually contribute to all of your Life Balance categories because it is a key way of ensuring that you are maintaining Life Balance and getting the maximum benefit from your Act $\times$ 6, Socialize $\times$ 5, Train $\times$ 4, and Ethos $\times$ 3 factorial activities. Its most important impact, however, is likely to be in the category of Personal and/or Spiritual Growth.

Each week: Reflect times two. A Balance Master sees life as a process of unfolding personal and spiritual growth. Reviewing progress through contemplation of the journey on a regular basis is essential to continued growth.

How and when will you Reflect?

15

Sabbath × 1

> **sab·bath** \\'sabəth\\ *n, often cap* : the day of rest and solemn
> assembly observed as sacred to God : a time of rest or repose :
> a cessation of effort, pain, or care

NOBODY WANTS TO TALK about the Sabbath. That may be because
so many of us were raised in childhoods in which the Sabbath in any of
its various but traditional forms was just one more restriction that
made life hard for active kids. For me, raised as a Roman Catholic, it
meant long Saturday-morning catechisms and a seemingly longer Sunday
Mass—in *Latin*, no less—held in concrete-block buildings that were hot
and stuffy in summer, cold and drafty in winter, and patrolled by an
army of eagle-eyed, wooden-ruler-bearing nuns looking for any opportunity to show us the errors of our ways.

It may be that we view ourselves somehow too sophisticated for
an idea as quaint as the "Sabbath," which in many minds seems as
though it should be relegated to the same corner as barn-raisings
and quilting bees. There may be truth in the belief of some that the

nicety of a Sabbath has been consigned to a back burner in many parts of postmodern society along with those seemingly dispensable concepts such as integrity, honesty, and compassion. We hear the word *Sabbath* and images of bearded, antediluvian patriarchs and stern-faced nineteenth-century Protestant ministers come to mind. These images are hardly in tune with the pounding rhythms of excess in the world as we experience it today.

It may just be that we've become overly busy. There was once a distinct line drawn between those times of activity that moved the business of life forward—our jobs, home chores, shopping, and so on—and the times when we didn't undertake such activities. For the most part, those periods of respite occurred on the weekends, which were also the traditional home of the Sabbath, regardless of the religious community to which one belonged. When I was growing up in the New York City metropolitan area, stores—*all* stores—were closed for business on Sundays, and many were closed by mid-afternoon on Saturday. This served as a natural break in our striving strides, giving us the opportunity to stop, pull back, relax, and take a few well-deserved deep breaths. Since what few activities there were revolved around houses of worship or spiritual communities of one form or another, it also provided the experience—or at least the opportunity—to contemplate the role of Spirit in our lives.

Today there is no getting away from the opportunities—and in some cases the demands—to move forward the "life under construction" portion of our activities. Shopping malls are open late into the evening nearly every day. Many supermarkets, drugstores, and even fast-food restaurants are open twenty-four hours. The great displacement of the ratio between wisdom, knowledge, and data, discussed in chapter 14, has impacted us in our work lives more than anywhere. Most of us simply cannot get away from our jobs at all—or at least not from the data-transmission portions of them and the immediate attention that the receipt of those transmissions demands. Cell phones, pagers, laptop computers, text messaging, faxes, PDAs, and a myriad of other electronic gadgets have effectively eliminated our ability to recluse ourselves from the demands of our workplaces. The very tools we created to give us more freedom instead have enslaved us beyond anyone's imagining.

I came face-to-face with this paradoxical conundrum at one point in my career when I worked at a global high-technology company. It was in the mid-1990s and early in my rotation as the chief of staff to the vice president who ran the division that designed and developed the miniature chip and board-level technology which enabled greater and greater functionality in laptop computers, PDAs, cell phones, and the like. I was sitting through a meeting in which one engineering manager after another was demonstrating the products and product ideas that were being worked on. "Just think," one proud manager exclaimed as his staff demonstrated a product whose functionality was technologically impressive at the time, "people will actually be able to receive faxes while they're at the beach!" At first, I couldn't believe my ears. Then I couldn't believe my *eyes* as I looked around and realized that I was the only one in the room horrified at the prospect of having my employer—or anyone, for that matter—forcibly downloading documents to me while I was attempting to relax at the seaside. I remember asking myself exactly why it was that I was helping these people! Since that day my impression is that technology has become only more invasive, infringing even further on our abilities to get away and experience something even akin to a Sabbath.

For whatever the reasons, the result of all these factors is that many of us are experiencing some degree of guilt around the idea of keeping a Sabbath while, at the same time, very few of us are doing anything about it. For some of us the guilt is based in old religious paradigms. For some the guilt is founded in an actual desire to spend time in a state of communion with Spirit and the inability to figure out how to do that with the demands on our time and attention. For others there is simply not enough time as it is to be with family and friends, and setting aside time for a Sabbath is perceived as exacerbating that problem.

That each of us may have difficult past and present experiences and beliefs regarding Sabbath doesn't make it any less relevant to our lives today. Indeed, the misunderstanding about the role of a Sabbath in our lives makes it even more difficult to experience Life Balance.

Simply put, individually and as a society we are out of the habit of Sabbath, and we *must* get back into that habit, albeit in a way that matches the circumstances of the lives we live today and not an idea of Sabbath borrowed from another century. We must bring the Sabbath back into our lives because its absence is a danger to us all.

To fully understand this, it is necessary once again to return to nature as an example. Everything in nature has a rhythm of activity and rest. The day and the night, the periods of active growth and dormancy in the plant world, the ebb and flow of the tides—nearly everything around us proclaims the need for a period of rest following a period of activity. Nothing in the world as we perceive it is "on" all the time.

Our ancestors looked at nature and accepted this wisdom as their own. They codified it into some of the earliest systems of religious laws and principles. The reminder to keep the Sabbath is the fourth of the Ten Commandments set out in the Book of Exodus and then repeated in the Book of Deuteronomy. In Hebrew, the word *shabbat* means to cease as well as to rest. The concept also exists in other religions, although the terminology is different. For example, the Buddhists speak of "taking refuge" in the Buddha nature. This is essentially the same as a spiritual Sabbath.

Observance of activity and rest on a cycle of seven was also observed as a method of agricultural husbandry in ancient Judea. A year of rest for the land was observed every seventh year by allowing the fields and vineyards to lie without tilling, sowing, pruning, or reaping from one autumn to the next in accordance with a Levitical commandment.

We humans, no less than the land, need rest. We need to re-gather our energies and restore our spirits by disengaging—for a short while, at least—from every demand for attention that is made on us. And this we no longer do.

But a true Sabbath represents more than simple withdrawal from the activities of the world. There needs to be a redirection of attention from the outer world to the inner world. The late Jewish philosopher Abraham Joshua Heschel, in his classic work *The Sabbath: Its Meaning for Modern Man*, wrote that the Sabbath is "a sanctuary in time" where people can escape from their constant struggle to acquire more and more power and possessions.

Wayne Muller here describes his view of the nature of Sabbath:

Sabbath is more than the absence of work; it is not just a day off, when we catch up on television or errands. It is the presence of something that arises when we consecrate a period of time to listen to what is most deeply beautiful, nourishing, or true. It is time consecrated with our attention, our mindfulness, honoring those quiet forces of grace or spirit that sustain and heal us.[1]

So, what does a twenty-first-century Sabbath experience look like? What is most amazing about this question is that its answer resides *in* the very question itself! While it may sound like a fool's riddle, the answer to the question "What does a twenty-first-century Sabbath experience look like?" is that "The twenty-first-century Sabbath experience looks like whatever it looks like (to you)!" This is so because the foundation of a Sabbath experience is not activity.

The magic ingredients that convert activities into Sabbath experiences are intention, willingness, mindfulness, and prayerfulness. First, you must intend for the experience to be your Sabbath. Second, you must be willing to experience your connection and communion with the spiritual side of your nature. Third, you need to remain mindful during your Sabbath that you are, indeed, participating in a Sabbath. ("Remember the Sabbath day, to keep it holy.") Lastly, you must maintain a prayerful heart and mind, meaning that you are open to receiving whatever gifts your keeping of the Sabbath will give to you.

Understanding that you have the ability to design your own Sabbath can be incredibly freeing, particularly to those of us for whom "Sabbath" was synonymous with "restriction." It is not what you do, it is not where you perform it, it is not who attends or joins you in the activity that makes it a Sabbath experience. There is no required time element—that is, it need not be a "day" in the normal meaning of the word because Sabbath happens out of time and out of normal space.

I have kept the Sabbath in houses of worship. I have kept the Sabbath at the beach, in the woods, in the desert. I have kept it in the sanctity of my own home and in hotels and motels when I am traveling. I have spent as much as a week at it and as little as an hour. Once you develop the habit of keeping the Sabbath, you will discover that where you keep it is actually in your heart.

Because of its spiritual nature, taking a Sabbath, of whatever duration, is also an opportunity to expand your experience of and connection to wisdom, as was described in chapter 14.

Note that keeping the Sabbath is not the same thing as reflection. It is not an opportunity for you to reflect on the successes and failures of the last week and your plan for the future. The Sabbath $\times$ 1 factorial is different from the Reflect $\times$ 2 factorial because the latter is about looking at your life—where it is, where it's been, where it's going—and the former is about looking at your place in the universe. This is a fine but clear distinction.

A Sabbath is an opportunity to consecrate a portion of your time and attention to experiencing the power of Spirit. To a certain extent, I suppose, it can be held akin to tithing, but a tithe of time and attention rather than a tithe of money or material possessions.

Make no restrictions on how you keep your Sabbath, but do arrange your life so that you do, in fact, keep the Sabbath. One important element of keeping a Sabbath is to establish some regular ritual for yourself and then to develop some degree of discipline in observing that ritual. Rituals need not be complicated. A ritual can be as simple as walking to the same place in your garden on a regular basis and allowing yourself to be filled by Spirit as best you are able. It can be as effortless as sitting on the beach for an hour or two to watch the power of the universe in the waves or to see the complexity of a single grain of sand. Spirit permeates our world everywhere. The purpose of a Sabbath is for you to come into communion with that Spirit in a way which leaves you somehow changed and refreshed. How we do that exactly does not matter, but do it we all must.

The Sabbath $\times$ 1 factorial is the complement of the Act $\times$ 6 factorial—indeed, they are more like opposites. You will discover that it is in your best interests not to perform Act $\times$ 6 activities on the same day as you keep your Sabbath—the energies run contrary to each other. However, participation in the activities for any of the other Balance Master's factorials on a Sabbath day is encouraged. These activities will have a different dimension when you perform them on days when you have rested in Sabbath.

You will find that a celebration of a Sabbath will create a foundation for you to experience renewed vigor on a weekly basis in every Life Balance category, but it will feel as though it is having the most direct effect in the category of Personal and/or Spiritual Growth.

Each week: Keep the Sabbath times one. A Balance Master recognizes that all life requires a rhythm of rest—a sacred time to take refuge from the work and process which life continually presents us.

What will be the discipline of your Sabbath?

EPILOGUE

THIS MAY BE THE END OF THIS BOOK, but at the same time, it is an important beginning. Hopefully it has become clear to you by this time that the process of creating and maintaining Life Balance is one you will have to continue, whether or not you plan to develop a degree of mastery of Life Balance. You will be dealing with Life Balance— enjoying its presence or suffering the consequences of its absence—for the rest of your life. Your life, you see, is just one command performance of your balancing-circus-bear act after another.

The investment you have made in reading this book, doing its exercises, and learning its principles will have been good *only* if you continue to adjust the path of your life's trajectory when you realize that, for whatever reason, you are not headed in the direction you want to be going. You can only do that if you have a monitoring system—a guidance system—in place. No one can monitor for you, no one can do those adjustments for you, and perhaps most importantly, no one can determine which direction is the right one for you, although, as you also probably know through experience, many will try to tell you that they do.

We need only look around to find more than enough examples of those who "lead lives of quiet desperation and go to the grave with the song still in them," as it was so perfectly and profoundly articulated by Henry David Thoreau. The only difference between those living in desperation and those living in fulfillment are their choices. The former make choices that do not result in their dreams becoming reality, or perhaps they remain unaware that the mechanism of change to move one's life ever closer to one's ideal is a process that can be consciously applied, but the result is the same. In short order they become trapped by their habits in a life lacking fulfillment.

You no longer have that excuse. You have the ability to join the ranks of those leading fulfilling lives because you now understand and can use "the process." Simply, that process consists of making a choice, seeing the consequences of that choice, choosing again if you don't like those consequences or think you can do better, reviewing the consequences of that re-choosing, choosing again, and so on. You now have new awareness and, better, you have the tools to do something about what you discover with your new awareness.

The Life Balance equation shows you the consequences of your present habits. Extrapolation from a recurring result to its underlying cause or causes is easy enough to do. The Habit Creation Cycle gives you everything you need to change your existing habits, and the Existing Habit Cycle will take it from there—naturally and effortlessly. The Balance Master's Factorial allows you to create a self-designed template for mastering balance to suit the specifics of your life. The

Balance Master's Factorial Scorecards make it easy to monitor your choices and activities and provide you with both tactical and strategic feedback. That feedback, in turn, permits you to change your future choices if you wish to get different results—results more in line with your dreams and desires.

The life you want lies within your grasp, but actively grasp it you must. Otherwise it will always remain beyond your reach, floating on the horizon like some tempting but frustrating mirage.

You have gifts to give to the people around you and to the world, but your ability to make good on that potential is circumscribed by the degree to which you fail to live life in pursuit of your own dreams. It matters not that those dreams will change over time—indeed, that some of them will change even before you have finished half your journey to their completion. As sage after sage has reminded us for millennia: It is not the destination that is important but the journey. You will discover that every completed step on your journey will be an inspiration to you and to others.

This book, then, has provided you with a road map and a few signposts for that journey. The rest is up to you. Do what you can—but do *everything you can*. What I expect you will discover after reading this book, applying its principles, and using its tools is that "everything you can" is actually everything you need.

Just as the oak exists in the tiny acorn, your limitless tomorrow is already in you.

Make it **grow!**

NOTES

CHAPTER 1

1. Snakehead Scientific Advisory Panel, *First Report to the Maryland Secretary of Natural Resources*, July 26, 2002; and Steve Early, *Updates on the Northern Snakehead Fish in Maryland*, Maryland Department of Natural Resources Fisheries Service, August 2002.

2. http://www.stress.org

3. http://www.stress.org

CHAPTER 2

1. For a complete discussion of outer-centered reality versus inner-centered reality, see the introduction to my earlier book, *Your Authentic Self: Be Yourself at Work* (Hillsboro, Ore.: Beyond Words Publishing, 2002).

CHAPTER 3

1. White Eagle, *Heal Thyself* (Liss, United Kingdom: Cambridge University Press, 1962, 1994), p. 23.

CHAPTER 5

1. *Webster's Third New International Dictionary, Unabridged.*

CHAPTER 7

1. For a full discussion of Monkey Mind and how to deal with it, see Chapter 8, "Manage Monkey Mind," in my earlier book, *Your Authentic Self: Be Yourself at Work* (Hillsboro, Ore.: Beyond Words Publishing, 2002).

CHAPTER 8

1. Additional supplies of cards can be purchased from The Spirit Employed Company either at its Web site *www.spiritemployed.com* or by contacting the company at 1-800-538-2001.

CHAPTER 9

1. Luciano Bernardi, "Effect of Rosary Prayer and Yoga Mantras on Autonomic Cardiovascular Rhythms: Comparative Study," *British Medical Journal* 323 (December 22–29, 2001): 1446–49.
2. Paramahansa Yogananda, *Metaphysical Meditations* (Los Angeles: Self-Realization Fellowship, 1932, 1994), pp. vi–vii.
3. For an additional discussion of the discipline of meditation and methods of its practice, see chapter 12, "Become Disciplined in Meditation," in my earlier book, *Your Authentic Self: Be Yourself at Work* (Hillsboro, Ore.: Beyond Words Publishing, 2002).
4. Michael Chender, "Meditation as a Radical Form of Inquiry," *Leverage* (an on-line journal published by Pegasus Communications), May 2000.

CHAPTER 10

1. Words and music by Fred Small. Copyright © 1983 by Pine Barrens Music (BMI). From the album *Everything Possible: Fred Small in Concert* (Flying Fish #625).

CHAPTER 14

1. For a complete discussion of outer-centered reality versus inner-centered reality, see the introduction to my earlier book, *Your Authentic Self: Be Yourself at Work* (Hillsboro, Ore.: Beyond Words Publishing, 2002).

CHAPTER 15

1. Wayne Muller, *Sabbath: Finding Rest, Renewal, and Delight in Our Busy Lives* (New York: Bantam Books, 1999), p. 8.

For more information about other books and tapes, or to invite Ric
for a speaking engagement, consultation, or facilitation of
a workshop, program, or retreat, please contact

The Spirit Employed Company

800-538-2001

or

408-264-9723

or

info@spiritemployed.com

You can access the Spirit Employed Web site at

www.spiritemployed.com

OUR CORPORATE MISSION

Inspire to Integrity

OUR DECLARED VALUES

We give to all of life as life has given us.
We honor all relationships.
Trust and stewardship are integral to fulfilling dreams.
Collaboration is essential to create miracles.
Creativity and aesthetics nourish the soul.
Unlimited thinking is fundamental.
Living your passion is vital.
Joy and humor open our hearts to growth.
It is important to remind ourselves of love.

To order or to request a catalog, contact

Beyond Words Publishing, Inc.
20827 N.W. Cornell Road, Suite 500
Hillsboro, OR 97124-9808
503-531-8700

You can also visit our Web site at *www.beyondword.com*
or e-mail us at *info@beyondword.com*.

FOCUS ITEMS FOR THE WEEK OF _____

YOUR FOCUS ITEMS:

YOUR PARTNER'S FOCUS ITEMS:

FOCUS ITEMS FOR THE WEEK OF _____

YOUR FOCUS ITEMS:

YOUR PARTNER'S FOCUS ITEMS:

7 M̲EDITATE						
7	6 A̲CT					
7	6	5 S̲OCIALIZE				
7	6	5	4 T̲RAIN			
7	6	5	4	3 E̲THOS		
7	6	5	4	3	2 R̲EFLECT	
7	6	5	4	3	2	1 S̲ABBATH

BALANCE MASTER'S FACTORIAL SCORECARD

7 M̲EDITATE						
7	6 A̲CT					
7	6	5 S̲OCIALIZE				
7	6	5	4 T̲RAIN			
7	6	5	4	3 E̲THOS		
7	6	5	4	3	2 R̲EFLECT	
7	6	5	4	3	2	1 S̲ABBATH